ELIZABETH M. BRIEL

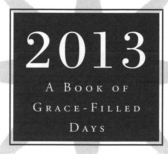

2013
A BOOK OF GRACE-FILLED DAYS

LOYOLA PRESS.
A JESUIT MINISTRY
Chicago

LOYOLA PRESS.
A JESUIT MINISTRY

3441 N. Ashland Avenue
Chicago, Illinois 60657
(800) 621-1008
www.loyolapress.com

Cover and interior design by Kathy Kikkert

Library of Congress Cataloging-in-Publication Data
Briel, Elizabeth M., 1967-
  2013 : a book of grace-filled days / Elizabeth M. Briel.
     p. cm.
  ISBN-13: 978-0-8294-3625-9
  ISBN-10: 0-8294-3625-1
1. Catholic Church--Prayers and devotions. 2. Church year--Prayers and devotions.
I. Title. II. Title: Twenty thirteen. III. Title: Two thousand thirteen.
  BX2170.C55B76 2012
  242'.3—dc23

                                                                              2012005682

Printed in the United States of America.
12 13 14 15 16 17 Bang 10 9 8 7 6 5 4 3 2 1

for my husband

INTRODUCTION

Two years before this book was released, years before you ever even picked it up, I was praying for you. That's the first thing to note. This work has been accomplished with you in mind, and as I've moved through each reading, I have carried you with me on every page. This book is truly, in every way, for you.

Second, you will meet some of my favorite friends, saints, authors. and theologians in these pages: Blessed John Paul II, Blessed John Henry Newman, Hans Urs von Balthasar, Caryll Houselander, St. Pio, Thomas Merton, St. Elizabeth, St. Anne, St. Joseph, St. John of the Cross, St. Ignatius of Loyola, an array of heavenly hosts, and others. Along with the Blessed Mother, I have sought their intercession on your behalf and mine. Many of them have produced extremely important theological works, and I hope you will seek them out if you do not already know them. Their work has enriched my life, my understanding of Scripture, meditation, prayer, and the spiritual life, and I trust these writings will do the same for you.

The third thing to keep in mind is this: though we may pray in solitude, in private as we are instructed to do by the Lord himself, we must not mistake ourselves for individuals pursuing our independent goals, but as members of the human family, and more specifically, the Church family, seeking the face of God and the salvation of all. "The future of the world," writes Blessed John Paul II in *Familiaris Consortio*, "passes through the family." Indeed, and prayer is one of the ways in which we enter the fullness of our spiritual kinship; here, on our knees, in private and in solitude, we discover we are not alone. In our sorrows, our joys, our every human experience—we are not alone. Some of the power of prayer—this communion with God—lies precisely in the shattering of the illusion of isolation.

But prayer with God's word is even more powerful still. Neal Lozano writes that "God's Word has the power to bring about what it means." Do you believe it? Do you want to believe it? God's word is powerful. God's word is true. And it was written, spoken into existence by the Trinity, with you in mind.

I sometimes drew from the work of others in a conscious effort to emphasize the communal nature of our faith and of our prayer life. Even though we may meditate in private and pray alone in our rooms with the door closed, away from the rest of the swirling world, every prayer we utter is joined in a perpetual, universal litany launched heavenward. May we draw on that communal power, that universal experience of the human heart that seeks the face of the Beloved who first seeks us.

St. John Vianney wrote that "Private prayer is like straw scattered here and there: If you set it on fire it makes a lot of little flames. But gather these straws into a bundle and light them, and you get a mighty fire, rising like a column into the sky; public prayer is like that."

Communal prayer is not easily extinguished. Though our prayer and meditation may not be public, it is *communal* in its way. This book, even if it was not consciously intended to do so, does bring all our minds to the same thought every day, and in this small way it becomes a communal prayer, one that I hope will resonate for you. Your heart is joined with mine and with so many others; we come together in that mystical way that only prayer can achieve and offer ourselves to Jesus to do with us, teach us, form us, heal us, and use us as he will.

May this be our little liturgy of the hours, our private prayer of the communal moments, whereby we come together, not in little flashes of flame, but bundled to set the world ablaze, a mighty, loving, fervent, familial fire.

Let's keep one another other in prayer.

DECEMBER 2

Jesus said to his disciples: "There will be signs in the sun, the moon and the stars, and on earth nations will be in dismay, perplexed by the roaring of the sea and the waves . . . But when these signs begin to happen, stand erect and raise your heads because your redemption is at hand."
—LUKE 21:25, 28

Jesus invites us, not to a posture of defeat and despair, but to a posture of hope and confident anticipation. Though his warnings are stern and very real—oh, how we must be reminded of our need for salvation. Advent calls us to an interior posture where we stand upright, heads raised in hope that God fulfills his promises.

Jeremiah 33:14—16
Psalm 25
1 Thessalonians 3:12—4:2
Luke 21:25–28, 34–36

In the days to come,
The mountain of the LORD's house
shall be established as the highest mountain
and raised above the hills.
All nations shall stream toward it.
—ISAIAH 2:2

Truth is attractive. It's beautiful and filling and irresistible. It draws in the heart, the mind, the whole person; and it raises us up to be established in high places, holy places. This is the promise in the days to come: to keep the Lord company in his house.

Isaiah 2:1–5
Psalm 122
Matthew 8:5–11

DECEMBER 4

Jesus rejoiced in the Holy Spirit . . . "I give you praise, Father, Lord of heaven and earth, for although you have hidden these things from the wise and the learned you have revealed them to the childlike."
—LUKE 10:21

A rejoicing Jesus may not be the most common image we have of him, but indeed, Jesus rejoices in the Holy Spirit and praises his Father, Lord of heaven and earth. He reveals himself to us in this childlike delight. A thankful, delighted heart is a flourishing heart.

Isaiah 11:1–10
Psalm 72
Luke 10:21–24

DECEMBER 5

Great crowds came to him, having with them the lame, the blind, the deformed, the mute, and many others. They placed them at his feet, and he cured them.
—MATTHEW 15:30

We place ourselves at the feet of Jesus with all our ills, fears, weaknesses, self-will, sin, and spiritual deformity. We place ourselves—blind, deaf, in pain—humble and low at his feet. This is the same Jesus of Matthew's Gospel, and he cures us, too.

Isaiah 25:6–10
Psalm 23
Matthew 15:29–37

DECEMBER 6

• ST. NICHOLAS, BISHOP •

A nation of firm purpose you keep in peace;
in peace, for its trust in you.
—ISAIAH 26:3

The psalmist cries out, "My heart is steadfast, oh God, my heart is steadfast." Where is my heart fixed? Are we fixed with firm purpose on the will of God? Do we know our purpose? Peace comes to those who fix their eyes on Jesus and trust in him.

Isaiah 26:1–6
Psalm 118
Matthew 7:21, 24–27

Wait for the LORD with courage;
Be stouthearted, and wait for the LORD.
—PSALM 27:14

All of Christian life is marked with the most profound
waiting. We are exhorted at every Mass with these words:
"as we wait in joyful hope for the coming of our Savior,
Jesus Christ." Every liturgical season seems to uphold the
stance of waiting. Why should the Church offer so many
opportunities to practice waiting? How well do we do it?
Do we wait with spiritual poise, a stout heart? What will it
mean for us when all this waiting is over?

Isaiah 29:17–24
Psalm 27
Matthew 9:27–31

DECEMBER 8

• THE IMMACULATE CONCEPTION OF THE BLESSED VIRGIN MARY •

In him we were also chosen, destined in accord with the purpose of the
One who accomplishes all things according to the intention of his will,
so that we might exist for the praise of his glory.
—EPHESIANS 1:11–12

Mary was chosen and prepared in a unique way, it's true.
She accomplished the will of the Father in an extraordinary
capacity. But one of the great gifts of her witness is to
remind us that we, also, have been chosen. We will be
prepared for our calling, and we will exist for God's greater
glory if we can make Mary's prayer our own: *be it done unto me*
according to your word.

Genesis 3:9–15, 20
Psalm 98
Ephesians 1:3–6, 11–12
Luke 1:26–38

DECEMBER 9

• SECOND SUNDAY OF ADVENT •

For God is leading Israel in joy by the light of his glory,
with his mercy and justice for company.
—BARUCH 5:9

What splendid company! Joy and glory, mercy and justice.
God can never be separated from these things; they are
essential to his essence. If you draw near to the Lord, you
draw near to his joy, justice, light, and mercy. Could we
want for better life companions? Is there anything keeping
us from seeking such friendship?

Baruch 5:1–9
Psalm 126
Philippians 1:4–6, 8–11
Luke 3:1–6

Say to those whose hearts are frightened:
Be strong, fear not!
Here is your God,
he comes with vindication;
with divine recompense
he comes to save you.
—ISAIAH 35:4

Do you believe it? What would you do if you weren't afraid? How would your life change if you knew in your heart that "he has come to save me"?

Isaiah 35:1–10
Psalm 85
Luke 5:17–26

It is not the will of your heavenly Father that one of these little ones be lost.
—MATTHEW 18:14

It is not the will of the Father that you should be left behind. No matter how far you may have strayed, no matter how distracted or tired you might be, no matter how insignificant you may believe you are, no matter how lost, abandoned, or forgotten you may feel—Jesus can find you anywhere and bring you home.

Isaiah 40:1–11
Psalms 96:1–2, 3, 10, 11–12, 13
Matthew 18:12–14

Your deed of hope will never be forgotten / by those who tell of the might of God.
—JUDITH 13:19

In *The Reed of God*, Caryll Houselander writes, "Advent is the season of the secret, the secret of the growth of Christ—of Divine love growing in silence." For Mary, "All her experience of the world about her was gathered to Christ growing in her." And for us, "we must believe that He is growing in our lives; we must believe it so firmly that we cannot help relating every thing, literally everything, to this almost incredible reality. Every work that we do should be a part of Christ being formed in us."

Zechariah 2:14–17 or Revelation 11:19; 12:1–6
Judith 13
Luke 1:26–38 or Luke 1:39–47

DECEMBER 13

Fear not, / I will help you . . . That all may see and know, / and observe and understand, / that the hand of the LORD has done this.
—ISAIAH 41:13, 20

St. Lucy is the patroness of those who are blind and those with eye troubles. But it is curious to note that her name means "light." God intends us to know him, to see him, to observe his mighty works and by doing so come to truly worship him. We need his light—the illumination of the sacraments, the saints, prayer, and study—to help show us God's saving hand constantly at work in our daily world.

St. Lucy, pray for our inner vision.

Isaiah 41:13–20
Psalm 145
Matthew 11:11–15

Friday

DECEMBER 14

• ST. JOHN OF THE CROSS, PRIEST AND DOCTOR OF THE CHURCH •

I, the LORD, your God, / teach you what is for your good, / and lead you on the way you should go.
—ISAIAH 48:17

John of the Cross writes, "What we need most to make progress is to be silent before this great God with our appetite and with our tongue, for the language he best hears is silent love." Advent is a season for quiet, silent movements of the Holy Spirit, who visits us in angels and dreams. Practice silence in order to learn the way that you should go.

Isaiah 48:17–19
Psalm 1
Matthew 11:16–19

DECEMBER 15

Elijah has already come, and they did not recognize him.
—MATTHEW 17:12

All the spiritual life is a movement toward deeper revelation—of revealing who we are and of being truly seen. God is constantly revealing himself to us and so often, we miss him entirely.

Give me better eyes, Lord. Remove from me those things that keep me from recognizing you, beholding you, and loving you in all that you are.

Sirach 48:1–4, 9–11
Psalm 80
Matthew 17:9–13

DECEMBER 16

• THIRD SUNDAY OF ADVENT •

God indeed is my savior;
I am confident and unafraid.
—ISAIAH 12:2

Fear can be a very powerful force. When fear threatens to
overtake me, I remember what a spiritual mentor once told
me: "I do not tell my God how big my problems are; I tell
my problems how big my God is." Amen. God is your
Savior, who will "rejoice over you with gladness and renew
you in his love." Be confident and unafraid; your strength
and courage is the Lord, who is near.

Zephaniah 3:14–18
Isaiah 12:2–3, 4, 5–6
Philippians 4:4–7
Luke 3:10–18

[O]f her was born Jesus who is called the Christ.
—MATTHEW 1:17

What are we to make of the various genealogies of Jesus?
We might simply concentrate on the fact that they point to
a longer, larger, and more vivid history than our own lives
and era. We are part of that lineage; we are part of salvation
history. We know he who was born of Mary: Jesus, the
Christ. And his name appears on our God-appointed
genealogies as his beloved sons and daughters.

Genesis 49:2, 8–10
Psalm 72
Matthew 1:1–17

DECEMBER 18

"Behold, the virgin shall be with child and bear a son,
and they shall name him Emmanuel,
which means, 'God is with us.'"
—MATTHEW 1:23

There's so much in a name. Has this one become too
familiar? Do I skip over it, or do I embrace it, kneel before
it because I recognize it as sacred and real?

Jeremiah 23:5–8
Psalm 72
Matthew 1:18–25

DECEMBER 19

An angel of the LORD appeared to the woman and said to her, "Though you are barren and have had no children, yet you will conceive and bear a son."
—JUDGES 13:3

Angels, angels everywhere. 'Tis the season for their appearances: to Mary, to Joseph, to the barren and the childless. They come announcing life where there should be none. They come proclaiming answered prayers and holy plans beyond all telling. They come and console us with 'do not be afraid, your prayer has been heard.'"

Judges 13:2–7, 24–25
Psalm 71
Luke 1:5–25

DECEMBER 20

"And behold, Elizabeth, your relative, has also conceived a son in her old age, and this is the sixth month for her who was called barren; for nothing will be impossible for God."
—LUKE 1:36–37

There are barren places in me just waiting to be made fruitful through God's grace. There are impossible obstacles ripe for removal.

Lord, make me your Elizabeth.

Isaiah 7:10–14
Psalm 24
Luke 1:26–38

Arise, my beloved, my beautiful one, and come! . . .
Let me see you,
let me hear your voice,
For your voice is sweet,
and you are lovely.
—SONG OF SONGS 2:13–14

This is the voice of the silent Christ of the Eucharist, the
invitation of adoration, intimate and personal. How long
has it been since you visited Jesus in adoration and let him
look on you with perfect love and holy delight?

Song of Songs 2:8–14 or Zephaniah 3:14–18
Psalm 33
Luke 1:39–45

DECEMBER 22

"My soul proclaims the greatness of the Lord; / my spirit rejoices in God my savior, / for he has looked upon his lowly servant. / From this day all generations will call me blessed: / the Almighty has done great things for me, / and holy is his Name. / He has mercy on those who fear him / in every generation. . . . / He has cast down the might from their thrones / and has lifted up the lowly. / He has filled the hungry with good things, / and the rich he has sent away empty. / He has come to the help of his servant Israel / for he remembered his promise of mercy, / the promise he made to our fathers, / to Abraham and his children for ever."
—LUKE 1:46–55

Amen. How might your Magnificat read?

1 Samuel 1:24–28
1 Samuel 2:1, 4–5, 6–7, 8
Luke 1:46–56

DECEMBER 23

• FOURTH SUNDAY OF ADVENT •

Blessed are you who believed that what was spoken to you by the Lord would be fulfilled.
—LUKE 1:45

Belief may not always be our problem. Discerning clearly the voice of the Lord in the cacophony of our culture and busy, daily lives may pose the greater challenge. How do we position ourselves best to hear the voice of God? What does it sound like? Prayer, the sacraments, meditating with Scripture, and a daily discipline of some bit of silence—these are good places to begin cultivating an ear that hears for the heart that believes.

Micah 5:1–4
Psalm 80
Hebrews 10:5–10
Luke 1:39–45

DECEMBER 24

In the tender compassion of our God / the dawn from on high shall break upon us, / to shine on those who dwell in darkness and the shadow of death, / and to guide our feet into the way of peace.
—LUKE 1:78–79

Tenderness and light. Guidance and peace. These the good gifts God has promised to us.

2 Samuel 7:1–5, 8b–12, 14a, 16
Psalm 89
Luke 1:67–79

DECEMBER 25

• THE NATIVITY OF THE LORD (CHRISTMAS) •

And the Word became flesh / and made his dwelling among us, / and we saw his glory, / and the glory as of the Father's only Son, / full of grace and truth.
—JOHN 1:14

"The Word became flesh." It's not an abstraction, an idea, a concept. Not a fairytale or theory. It's a *him*, a baby, a king, the Messiah, fragile and innocent and real entering into human history quietly in the night. He is Jesus.

Vigil:	**Dawn:**
Isaiah 62:1–5	Isaiah 62:11–12
Psalm 89	Psalm 97
Acts 13:16–17, 22–25	Titus 3:4–7
Matthew 1:1–25	Luke 2:15–20
Midnight:	**Day:**
Isaiah 9:1–6	Isaiah 52:7–10
Psalm 96	Psalm 98
Titus 2:11–14	Hebrews 1:1–6
Luke 2:1–14	John 1:1–18 or 1:1–5, 9–14

DECEMBER 26

• ST. STEPHEN, THE FIRST MARTYR •

Into your hands I commend my spirit;
You will redeem me, O LORD, O faithful God.
I will rejoice and be glad because of your mercy.
—PSALM 31:5, 7

"Father, into your hands, I commend my spirit." We tend to
think of this prayer as marking the end of life, the end of
our service, but I wonder if we might incorporate it into the
beginning of every day, to the start of our works of service.
"To commend" means to entrust for care or preservation, to
be remembered with kindness. Today, entrust yourself to
Jesus and be glad for his mercy.

Acts 6:8–10; 7:54–59
Psalm 31
Matthew 10:17–22

So Peter and the other disciple went out and came to the tomb. They both ran, but the other disciple ran faster than Peter and arrived at the tomb first; he bent down and saw the burial clothes there, but did not go in.
—JOHN 20:4–5

Here's a wonderful feast tossed into our Advent reflections: the moment of Easter Resurrection. There is something so lovely and unleashed in John, which carried him more swiftly to the tomb. And yet he does not go in. He allows Peter to enter first. Great love can make us as light and free as the wind. It can also make us as still and gentle as a dove, supple to the significant movements of the spirit that will reach forward into all human history.

1 John 1:1–4
Psalm 97
John 20:2–8

Friday

DECEMBER 28

• THE HOLY INNOCENTS, MARTYRS •

"A voice was heard in Ramah,
sobbing and loud lamentation;
Rachel weeping for her children,
and she would not be consoled,
since they were no more."
—MATTHEW 2:18

There are many ways to murder innocence. Through the intercession of the Holy Innocents, today let us pray for all those whose lives or innocence has been lost through abuse, neglect, or cultural pressures. Let us thank our generous God who can restore all that has been lost, who can restore us to a proper childlike wonder at his goodness and the merciful gifts of life and eternal love.

1 John 1:5–2:2
Psalm 124
Matthew 2:13–18

DECEMBER 29

• ST. THOMAS BECKET, BISHOP AND MARTYR •

[A]nd you yourself a sword will pierce.
—LUKE 2:35

In this season of light and joy, a shadow is cast. What do
we make of this presentiment? Is it possible that our joy is
made complete, made mature and whole, only when taken
in the context of eternity? Is it possible that joy is simply
sorrow and suffering all grown up? Is it possible that
whatever suffering we may be experiencing is tied to our
future joy, like the muddy, hidden roots that anchor a
strong and thriving tree?

1 John 2:3–11
Psalm 96
Luke 2:22–35

*Beloved: See what love the Father has bestowed on us that we may be
called the children of God. And so we are.*
—1 JOHN 3:1

Celebrating this feast may not be easy for everyone. Those
among us who have grown up in families that are anything
but holy may struggle to imagine a loving Father who calls
his children "beloved." Today I pray for all families,
especially those in crisis, those who struggle to honor and
love one another, those who may feel they have no family
at all. May they be reminded by our kindness and witness
that they are beloved by God.

Sirach 3:2–6, 12–14
Psalm 128 or 84
1 John 3:1–2, 21–24 or Colossians 3:12–21 or 3:12–17
Luke 2:41–52

⇒ 29 ⇐

DECEMBER 31

All things came to be through him, / and without him nothing came to be. / What came to be through him was life, / and this life was the light of the human race; / the light shines in the darkness, / and the darkness has not overcome it.
—JOHN 1:3–4

"The darkness has not overcome it." It may be difficult to believe this some days, with war, natural disasters, illness, starvation, divorce, abortion, greed, and every kind of sin and fear rampaging across the face of the earth. But this we also know: the word of God is true. Where will you find the light in the darkness today? Look for it. Expect it. Trust it. Let Jesus surprise you and strengthen *you* to be a light in the new year ahead.

1 John 2:18–21
Psalms 96
John 1:1–18

JANUARY 1

• MARY, MOTHER OF GOD •

And Mary kept all these things,
reflecting on them in her heart.
—LUKE 2:19

This image of Mary—hidden, quiet, pondering, and
private—we may be tempted to diminish or downplay. We
might interpret her as a woman subdued by the oppression
of patriarchal rule, hushed and humbled by powers beyond
her control. Our culture has grown too fond of power,
noise, and constant motion. But cultivating the kind of
quiet, private interiority that Mary shows us is indicative of
a woman self-possessed and spiritually poised, a woman
who lives with courage and great depth of heart.

Numbers 6:22–27
Psalm 67
Galatians 4:4–7
Luke 2:16–21

JANUARY 2

• ST. BASIL THE GREAT AND ST. GREGORY NAZIANZEN, BISHOPS AND DOCTORS OF THE CHURCH •

All the ends of the earth have seen
the salvation by our God.
—PSALM 98:3

This month of readings is riddled with reminders of God's power, abundance, generosity, grandeur, provision, faithfulness, and mercy. Where are you seeing the saving power of God in the world, in your family, in your workplace, in you? Stand watch. Be on the lookout for God's saving, abundant, and generous hand.

1 John 2:22–28
Psalm 98
John 1:19–28

JANUARY 3

• THE MOST HOLY NAME OF JESUS •

John the Baptist saw Jesus coming toward him and said, "Behold, the Lamb of God, who takes away the sin of the world."
—JOHN 1:29

Dear St. John, how did you know him? Was it the way he walked, the way he looked, something in his eyes, his posture, his person? How did you know this was the Lamb of God, your Savior long-awaited, the One for whom you prepared the way, the One you would baptize in a river, and the One upon whom the Spirit of God would descend? Dear St. John, pray for me that I may see him, behold him, and love him as you do.

1 John 2:29—3:6
Psalm 98
John 1:29–34

He first found his own brother Simon and told him, "We have found the Messiah . . ." Then he brought him to Jesus. Jesus looked at him and said, "You are Simon the son of John; you will be called Cephas," which is translated Peter.
—JOHN 1:41–42

It was their first meeting—Peter and Jesus. What must have been going through Peter's mind?

Lord, take me back to our first meeting, our first encounter, when you gave me a new name and I realized that I had found the Messiah. Refresh me with the wonder of your loving revelation.

1 John 3:7–10
Psalm 98
John 1:35–42

JANUARY 5

If someone who has worldly means sees a brother in need and refuses him compassion, how can the love of God remain in him? Children, let us love not in word or speech but in deed and truth.
—1 JOHN 3:17

A sociologist who studies contemporary slavery once told me that if you own your own car, you are in the top 3 percent of the world's population in terms of wealth. If you own your own home, you're in the top 1 percent. Maybe we need to remind ourselves of our means and give them away when and how we can so that the love of God can tend to those in need through us—our hands, our presence, our selves.

1 John 3:11–21
Psalm 100
John 1:43–51

They were overjoyed at seeing the star, and on entering the house they saw the child with Mary his mother. They prostrated themselves and did him homage. Then they opened their treasures and offered him gifts of gold, frankincense, and myrrh.
—MATTHEW 2:10–11

The three wise men were overjoyed at finding Jesus. They prostrated themselves, opened their treasures, and offered gifts befitting the Messiah. Am I overjoyed when I find Jesus throughout my day? Do I offer him my treasures: skills, prayers, suffering, relationships, desires, will, heart? Do I offer them on bended knee, in humility and homage, offering gifts fit for a King?

Isaiah 60:1–6
Psalm 72
Ephesians 3:2–3, 5–6
Matthew 2:1–12

JANUARY 7

• ST. RAYMOND OF PENYAFORT, PRIEST •

The LORD said to me, "You are my Son;"
this day I have begotten you.
Ask of me and I will give you
the nations for an inheritance
and the end of the earth for your possession.
—PSALM 2:7–8

In accepting Jesus—and our position as children of
God—we accept a royal inheritance. In doing so, we turn
our hearts, minds, and lives toward an abundance and lavish
love poured out upon us from heaven and drawing us ever
into eternity.

1 John 3:22—4:6
Psalm 2
Matthew 4:12–17, 23–25

They all ate and were satisfied.
—MARK 6:42

Moved with pity, Jesus meets the needs of the crowd in every way, spiritually and physically, going above and beyond all expectation or hope. The story of the fishes and the loaves points directly to the Eucharist—the Eucharist is the meal where we come, weary and not enough, so deeply in need. The Eucharist is where all eat and are satisfied.

Take every disappointment and every dissatisfaction to the altar meal and allow Jesus to make it eucharistic.

1 John 4:7–10
Psalm 72
Mark 6:34–44

JANUARY 9

There is no fear in love, but perfect love drives out fear because fear has to do with punishment, and so one who fears is not yet perfect in love.
—1 JOHN 4:18

Jesus frequently reminded his flock: be not afraid. In recent years I have struggled seriously with my health. It occurs to me that the only real disease I suffer from, outside of sinfulness, is fear: fear of the future, fear of what might happen, fear of future suffering. Jesus, save me from this terrible disease of fear. Perfect me in love. I will be careful to remember today that whatever trouble I may face, you are not nervous, and you are not afraid.

1 John 4:11–18
Psalm 72
Mark 6:45–52

JANUARY 10

For the love of God is this, that we keep his commandments. And his commandments are not burdensome, for whoever is begotten by God conquers the world.
—1 JOHN 5:3–4

When I find the demands and commands of Christian life burdensome, I might take a "love inventory": how well am I loving? As the Swiss theologian Hans Urs von Balthasar writes in *Christian State of Life*, "love does not inquire how far it *must* go, but how far it *may* go. We do not have to urge love to action, but rather to restrain it."

Lord, ever expand my capacity to love.

1 John 4:19—5:4
Psalm 72
Luke 4:14–22

[B]ut he would withdraw to deserted places to pray.
—LUKE 5:16

The healing of Jesus seems to flow endlessly, gracefully into all who seek it, even those of us filled to the brim with disease, whether spiritual or physical. But his healing work was surrounded with prayer. How much more must our works be surrounded and supported by prayer. When was the last time I withdrew to a deserted place to pray, to simply keep Jesus' close and quiet company?

1 John 5:5–13
Psalm 147
Luke 5:12–16

He must increase; I must decrease.
—JOHN 3:30

Is becoming a disciple of Jesus' about disappearing, about our disintegration? Isn't it good that I exist? There's a big difference between self-annihilation and self-donation. Perhaps John's words are another way of saying that our will must conform more and more to the Father's, that we must increase in self-gift, that the work God has given us to do must be fueled not by our ego or self-will but by God's love and our gratitude in being loved so well.

1 John 5:14–21
Psalm 149
John 3:22–30

JANUARY 13

• THE BAPTISM OF THE LORD •

After . . . Jesus . . . had been baptized and was praying, heaven was
opened and the Holy Spirit descended upon him in bodily form like a
dove. And a voice came from heaven, "You are my beloved Son; with
you I am well pleased."
—LUKE 3:21–22

The form of a dove—such a mild and lovely creature,
fragile, even vulnerable. It is a vivid reminder that often the
work of the Holy Spirit in us, this gift given to us as
beloved of the Father, is gentle and delicate, often coming
while we pray. It descends light as air, quiet like a whisper.
The movement of the Spirit in us can be subtle refinement
at its most divine.

Isaiah 42:1–4, 6–7 or 40:1–5, 9–11
Psalm 29 or 104
Acts 10:34–38 or Titus 2:11–14; 3:4–7
Luke 3:15–16, 21–22

JANUARY 14

Jesus came to Galilee proclaiming the Gospel of God . . . "Repent, and believe in the Gospel."
—MARK 1:14–15

Repentance. It's a strong word we tend to reject for its implications—like "fire and brimstone"—as though we have outgrown such a notion. As though we've become so sophisticated we no longer need to repent. But Christ's message comes in an important twofold combination: repent and believe. The Gospel message does not end with our repentance but with our believing in the saving grace of Jesus. I will never out-advance the need for grace.

Hebrews 1:1–6
Psalm 97
Mark 1:14–20

JANUARY 15

What is man that you are mindful of him?
—PSALM 8:4

Lord, today may I feel your greatness in contrast to my littleness; your awesome power set against my feeble humanity; your generous and lavish gift of life, that I may love you and know you more.

Hebrews 2:5–12
Psalm 8
Mark 1:21–28

⇒ 45 ⇐

JANUARY 16

Give thanks to the LORD, invoke his name; / make known among the nations his deeds. / Sing to him, sing his praise, / proclaim all his wondrous deeds.
—PSALM 105:1

In *Salvifici doloris*, Blessed John Paul II wrote that suffering unleashes love. Yes, and gratitude unleashes spiritual joy. A mentor trained me in the habit of making daily gratitude lists. It taught me what seems to be an obvious lesson now: on even the darkest days, there is always reason to give thanks to God. What goes on your gratitude list today? Long or short, you have a list just waiting to unleash the joy of heaven upon you.

Hebrews 2:14–18
Psalm 105
Mark 1:29–39

⇒ 46 ⇐

JANUARY 17

A leper came to him and kneeling down begged him and said, "If you wish, you can make me clean." Moved with pity, he stretched out his hand, touched the leper and said to him, "I do will it. Be made clean." The leprosy left him immediately, and he was made clean.
—MARK 1:40–42

Lord, here I am, on my knees and asking with my whole heart. Things I've carried too long—heavy and dark and impossible—have disfigured me, body and soul. Just like the leper, I know that, if you wish it, you can heal me, too.

Hebrews 3:7–14
Psalm 95
Mark 1:40–45

Do not forget the works of the Lord!
—PSALM 78:7

It's almost humorous—how often Scripture reminds us of God's faithfulness. Scripture is replete with examples of his abundant gifts: his forgiveness, mercy, and provision. We tend to be a forgetful people. Long ago, I started a prayer journal, and I frequently page through one of the many volumes to see how the Lord has answered my prayers, big and small, complicated and simple.

Jesus, I remember your works; I remember you.

Hebrews 4:1–5, 11
Psalm 78
Mark 2:1–12

We do not have a high priest who is unable to sympathize with our weaknesses, but one who has similarly been tested in every way, yet without sin. So let us confidently approach the throne of grace to receive mercy and to find grace for timely help.
—HEBREWS 4:15–16

It is a glorious image on which to meditate, the throne of grace where mercy and help are bestowed upon those who approach with confidence in God's word. See yourself there. What grace, what mercy would you ask for today? Approach with confidence in your heart. God knows you perfectly, in your weaknesses and strengths. And God's word is true, living, and effective: "your words, Lord, are Spirit and life."

Hebrews 4:12–16
Psalm 19
Mark 2:13–17

JANUARY 20

"Do whatever he tells you."
—JOHN 2:5

Your gifts may be simple: teaching, hospitality, wisdom, writing, prayer, poverty, celibacy, administration, craftsmanship. But each is given to build up the Body of Christ. Who needs your gifts? Identify your gifts and give them away in love; this will be the surest way to "do whatever he tells you."

Isaiah 62:1–5
Psalm 96
1 Corinthians 12:4–11
John 2:1–11

⇒ 50 ⇐

JANUARY 21

• ST. AGNES, VIRGIN AND MARTYR •

Son though he was, he learned obedience from what he suffered.
—HEBREWS 5:8

It is only natural to avoid suffering when possible, but every life will be marked by it. How do we respond to it? What do we do with it?

Lord, your humanity was made perfect through suffering, and so must mine be. Teach me everything I can possibly learn through my suffering; let none of it go to waste.

Hebrews 5:1–10
Psalm 110
Mark 2:18–22

JANUARY 22

*Hold fast to the hope that lies before us. This we have as an anchor of
the soul, sure and firm, which reaches into the interior behind the veil,
where Jesus has entered on our behalf as forerunner, become high priest
forever according to the order of Melchizedek.*
—HEBREWS 6:18–20

Like the word *love*, *hope* has been hijacked and forced into
labor by those who do not understand it in any theological
sense. Our hope is not anchored in human inventions or
technology, in the stock market, in our bank accounts or
bodies. Our hope is anchored in the very soul of Christ.
Our hope is of an eternal order. Nothing temporal can
substitute for the sure reach of Jesus, which goes before us
and draws us into eternity.

Hebrews 6:10–20
Psalm 111
Mark 2:23–28

There was a man there who had a withered hand . . . Jesus said to the man, "Stretch out your hand." He stretched it out and his hand was restored. The Pharisees went out and immediately took counsel with the Herodians against him to put him to death.
—MARK 3:1, 5–6

Hardness of heart always destroys. It's always plotting, even if subtly, to kill any healing love around it. It can be a difficult and painful task to admit our own proclivities for hardness of heart—the little indulgent jealousies, the private acts of willfulness, the ways we lie to ourselves or others, gossip, criticize or judge. But Jesus wants to heal those specific places within us.

Will we let him?

Hebrews 7:1–3, 15–17
Psalm 110
Mark 3:1–6

Thursday

JANUARY 24

• ST. FRANCIS DE SALES, BISHOP AND DOCTOR OF THE CHURCH •

Sacrifice or oblation you wished not,
but ears open to obedience you gave me.
—PSALM 40:7

My faith life, while engaging, is not all that dramatic. It's rather commonplace, my little daily creeping toward holiness. I fall down frequently. Salesian spirituality is a comfort for its emphasis on meekness, a quiet faith. St. Francis would not be impressed by emotional, tumultuous conversions. Rather, for him, it was in the daily things, the gentle promises, the small steps made in love and faithfulness that bring us daily into the kingdom.

Hebrews 7:25—8:6
Psalm 40
Mark 3:7–12

⇒ 54 ⇐

I persecuted this Way to death, binding both men and women and delivering them to prison.
—ACTS 22:4

It is good to remember Paul's story, good to be reminded that though he persecuted Christians, threw them into prison, and had them killed, he went on to become God's chosen instrument. We are all capable of such conversion. No matter what we've done or how violently we may have resisted the Lord, it is possible to change and to become the instrument of heaven.

Acts 22:3–16 or 9:1–22
Psalm 117
Mark 16:15–18

I remind you to stir into flame the gift of God that you have through the imposition of my hands. For God did not give us a spirit of cowardice but rather of power and love and self-control.
—2 TIMOTHY 1:6–7

Paul wrote these words while imprisoned in Rome. As he awaits his execution, he exhorts Timothy to embrace his ministry with a greater awareness of God's touch on Timothy's life. The literal imposition of hands is reserved for priests and deacons, but we are all called to stir into flame the good gifts of God, to witness to God's love with power and poise.

Let's pray for Church leadership.

2 Timothy 1:1–8 or Titus 1:1–5
Psalm 47
Mark 3:20–21

JANUARY 27

Ezra blessed the LORD, the great God, and all the people, their hands raised high, answered, "Amen, amen!" Then they bowed down and prostrated themselves before the LORD, their faces to the ground.
—NEHEMIAH 8:6

For all the fumblings they may have undertaken, the Israelites put their whole being into their relationship with God; they were unafraid of full-bodied worship, full-hearted faith.

What does my worship look like?

Nehemiah 8:2–4, 5–6, 8–10
Psalm 19
1 Corinthians 12:12–30 or 12:12–14, 27
Luke 1:1–4; 4:14–21

How shall a young man be faultless in his way?
By keeping to your words.
With all my heart I seek you;
Let me not stray from your commands.
—PSALM 119:10–11

St. Thomas said, "To one who has faith, no explanation is
necessary. To one without faith, no explanation is possible."
We may recognize this doctor of the church chiefly for his
mind, but he never abandoned his heart. He knew that
wisdom did not exist solely in the mind, but rather, "takes
up where knowledge leaves off."

Wisdom 7:7–10, 15–16
Psalm 119
Matthew 23:8–12

I have waited, waited for the LORD,
and he stooped toward me.
—PSALM 40:2

God is always coming our way, filling the gap between us,
taking our little effort and filling in the rest.

Hebrews 10:1–10
Psalm 40
Mark 3:31–35

JANUARY 30

*"I will put my laws in their hearts,
and I will write them upon their minds."*
—HEBREWS 10:16

There is an essential marriage at work here: heart and mind in union, faith and reason side by side, neither left to their own devices. We are invited to fall in love with the Truth.

Hebrews 10:11–18
Psalm 110
Mark 4:1–20

JANUARY 31

• ST. JOHN BOSCO, PRIEST •

Let us hold unwaveringly to our confession that gives us hope, for he who made the promise is trustworthy.
—HEBREWS 10:23

The promises of God are great, the healing love of Christ almost too good to be true. How can anyone love us so much—enough to suffer unjust accusations, to die on a cross, abandoned by so many?

We know God's word is true and that he who made the promise is trustworthy.

Hebrews 10:19–25
Psalm 24
Mark 4:21–25

FEBRUARY 1

Take delight in the LORD,
And he will grant you your heart's requests.
—PSALM 37:4

The Lord comes and asks me, "Beloved, I wish to grant you
your heart's desire." Does it sound too good to be true?
What is your heart's desire? The more I know of Jesus, the
more I know that he keeps his promises; he hears every
prayer and understands every longing. There is nothing of
my heart I cannot bring to him and entrust to his
perfect care.

Hebrews 10:32–39
Psalm 37
Mark 4:26–34

FEBRUARY 2

• THE PRESENTATION OF THE LORD •

When they had fulfilled all the prescriptions of the law of the Lord, they returned to Galilee, to their own town of Nazareth. The child grew and became strong, filled with wisdom; and the favor of God was upon him.
—LUKE 2:32

There may be no simpler way to grow in character than to present ourselves daily to God, to honor his commandments in simplicity and humility, as the Holy Family did. Joseph and Mary weren't a quaint little couple, mindlessly obeying a tradition; their holiness was attended by the righteous and the prophets. For their loving, simple fiat they were entrusted with the care of the King, the favored One, the light of revelation to the Gentiles.

Malachi 3:1–4
Psalm 24
Hebrews 2:14–18
Luke 2:22–40 or 2:22–32

FEBRUARY 3

And if I have the gift of prophecy, and comprehend all mysteries and all knowledge; if I have all faith so as to move mountains, but do not have love, I am nothing.
—1 CORINTHIANS 13:2

Conversion is not simply a matter of knowledge; it is a matter of love. Blessed John Paul II has written that "the successes of science and technology . . . can also lead to a gradual loss of sensitivity for man, that is for what is *essentially human.*" That is, love for one another. Though I may be tempted to live in my head, Lord, let me never forget that love is the greatest of these.

Jeremiah 1:4–5, 17–19
Psalm 71
1 Corinthians 12:31—13:13 or 13:4–13
Luke 4:21–30

⇒ 64 ⇐

FEBRUARY 4

"Unclean spirit, come out of the man!"
—MARK 5:8

We all have our demons—sins or fears that haunt us. They may not be as dramatic or as literal as those who possess the man in today's Gospel reading, but they are just as present and just as capable of blocking us from living in our right minds with a clean heart. The same power that healed the demoniac two thousand years ago is available to me, right now. Jesus, come and free me; make my heart clean.

Hebrews 11:32–40
Psalm 31
Mark 5:1–20

FEBRUARY 5

• ST. AGATHA, VIRGIN AND MARTYR •

*Let us rid ourselves of every burden and sin that clings to us and
persevere in running the race that lies before us while keeping our eyes
fixed on Jesus.*
—HEBREWS 12:1–2

May this phrase keep me close company, especially when I
am tempted to despair: fix your eyes on Jesus. We
remember the woman with the hemorrhage who reached
for his cloak and the little girl everyone presumed to be
dead. Jesus continues to come back to us, always with
power to heal, ever available to free us of our clinging
burdens and sin. If only we reach for him and keep our eyes
fixed on him.

Hebrews 12:1–4
Psalm 22
Mark 5:21–43

FEBRUARY 6

• ST. PAUL MIKI AND COMPANIONS, MARTYRS •

The LORD has done great things for us,
and we are filled with joy.
—PSALM 126:3

While hanging from a cross, Br. Paul Miki, a Jesuit and native of Japan, preached to those who had gathered to watch him along with twenty-six of his companions. He implored them to "Ask Christ to help you to become happy. I obey Christ. After Christ's example I forgive my persecutors. . . . I ask God to have pity on all, and I hope my blood will fall on my fellow men as a fruitful rain."

Galatians 2:19–20
Psalm 126
Matthew 28:16–20

FEBRUARY 7

He instructed them to take nothing for the journey but a walking stick—no food, no sack, no money in their belts.
—MARK 6:8

Lord, help me loosen my grip on all that is unessential. Let me keep my hands empty, open, and soft, to receive and give as you would have me do. Show me where in my daily journey I may rely more on you and less on the things around me to bring a sense of safety and security.

Hebrews 12:18–19, 21–24
Psalm 48
Mark 6:7–13

Your presence, O LORD, I seek.
—PSALM 27:9

In everyone I encounter today, oh Lord, I will seek your face. In the workings of my day, oh Lord, I will seek you. In your word, your works, the holy Mass, the sacraments, the sunrise, and the sunset, Lord, I seek you.

Hebrews 13:1–8
Psalm 27
Mark 6:14–29

FEBRUARY 9

Obey your leaders and defer to them, for they keep watch over you and will have to give an account.
—HEBREWS 13:17

It is difficult to be an effective leader. Do I pray for my Church, my civic and community leaders at least as often as I criticize them? Do I help keep them accountable, or do I ignore my responsibilities?

Hebrews 13:15–17, 20–21
Psalm 23
Mark 6:30–34

FEBRUARY 10

But by the grace of God I am what I am, and his grace to me has not been ineffective.
—1 CORINTHIANS 15:10

These are the words of a martyr and saint. They should give us great confidence and courage that God is always actively working in us. In every Mass, every holy hour, every minor sacrifice we make out of love, every small prayer we utter throughout our day, God-given graces (saint-making graces) are ushered straight to the heart.

Isaiah 6:1–2a, 3–8
Psalm 138
1 Corinthians 15:1–11 or 15:3–8, 11
Luke 5:1–11

FEBRUARY 11

• OUR LADY OF LOURDES •

They laid the sick in the marketplaces and begged him that they might touch only the tassel on his cloak; and as many as touched it were healed.
—MARK 6:56

We are asked to extend the same healing to all those around us. Caryll Houselander called it "Christing the world." When we live a sacramental life, when we let the Holy Spirit work through us, the healing touch we might offer the world is not ours, but the touch of Jesus Christ, Healer.

Genesis 1:1–19
Psalm 104
Mark 6:53–56

FEBRUARY 12

*So God blessed the seventh day and made it holy, because on it he rested
from all the work he had done in creation.*
—GENESIS 2:3

It's Tuesday. Sometime between now and Sunday, make
concrete plans to spend time in Sabbath rest on Sunday:
resting in God's word, resting in the company of loved
ones, resting in the beauty of creation, resting in
contemplation of God's promises fulfilled and prayers
answered. Rest with God by remembering his mighty works
and faithfulness in your life.

Genesis 1:20–2:4a
Psalm 8
Mark 7:1–13

Even now, says the LORD,
return to me with your whole heart,
with fasting, and weeping and mourning.
—JOEL 2:12

Return to me with *your whole heart*. Are there pieces I am holding back? Little pockets I'm protecting?

Lord, I hear you. This Lent, I want to bring my whole heart to you and allow you to move me, wherever that may lead me, whatever the cost.

Joel 2:12–18
Psalm 51
2 Corinthians 5:20—6:2
Matthew 6:1–6, 16–18

FEBRUARY 14

• ST. CYRIL, MONK • ST. METHODIUS, BISHOP •

"If anyone wishes to come after me, he must deny himself and take up his cross daily and follow me. For whoever wishes to save his life will lose it, but whoever loses his life for my sake will save it."
—LUKE 9:23–24

Christian life is filled with such dynamic tensions—God and man, Virgin and mother, faith and reason. These paradoxes test our willfulness and push back against the worldly notion that giving ourselves to God is really mental illness and not life-giving love.

Deuteronomy 30:15–20
Psalm 1
Luke 9:22–25

FEBRUARY 15

Have mercy on me, O God, in your goodness;
in the greatness of your compassion wipe out my offense.
Thoroughly wash me from my guilt
and of my sin cleanse me.
—PSALM 51:3–4

Who among us has not felt the weight of our faults and offenses? It's very easy to talk myself out of admitting my own sin, to pretty it up with self-justification or self-pity. May I never lose sight of how much I need God's mercy.

Isaiah 58:1–9
Psalm 51
Matthew 9:14–15

FEBRUARY 16

If you hold back your foot on the sabbath
from following your own pursuits on my holy day;
If you call the sabbath a delight,
and the LORD's holy day honorable;
If you honor it by not following your ways,
seeking your own interests, or speaking with malice—
Then you shall delight in the LORD,
and I will make you ride on the heights of the earth;
I will flourish you with the heritage of Jacob, your father,
for the mouth of the LORD has spoken.
—ISAIAH 58:13–14

Tomorrow is Sunday. What's your plan for Sabbath rest?

Isaiah 58:9b–14
Psalm 86
Luke 5:27–32

FEBRUARY 17

• FIRST SUNDAY OF LENT •

Filled with the Holy Spirit, Jesus returned from the Jordan and was led by the Spirit into the desert for forty days, to be tempted by the devil. He ate nothing during those days, and when they were over he was hungry.
—LUKE 4:1–2

During Lent, Jesus' full humanity is revealed. We see it in his passion and death, but also in this altercation with the evil one who tempts Jesus when he is filled with human hunger. In Lent, we ask that our own temptations be revealed, to help us better understand and avoid them, and to respond the way Jesus responded to temptation: with faith in God's word and confidence that the Holy Spirit will lead us no matter how weak we are.

Deuteronomy 26:4–10
Psalm 91
Romans 10:8–13
Luke 4:1–13

*You shall not bear hatred for your brother in your heart. Though you
may have to reprove him, do not incur sin because of him. Take no
revenge and cherish no grudge against your fellow countrymen. You
shall love your neighbor as yourself. I am the LORD.*
—LEVITICUS 19:17–18

Does this feel impossible—letting go of grudges? Does it
seem too much to ask of a mere mortal who's been truly
injured? Blessed Mother Teresa used to say that if you knew
everyone's story, you'd love everyone. If we keep trying to
understand those who have offended us, if we keep praying
for them even if we don't yet mean it, if we keep in mind
that—just like you and me—everyone has a story to tell,
we'll get there.

Leviticus 19:1–2, 11–18
Psalm 19
Matthew 25:31–46

FEBRUARY 19

The LORD is close to the brokenhearted;
and those who are crushed in spirit he saves.
—PSALM 34:18

To every crushed spirit and broken heart: over you, the
Spirit hovers. Tending, tending.

Isaiah 55:10–11
Psalm 34
Matthew 6:7–15

FEBRUARY 20

When God saw by their actions how they turned from their evil way, he repented of the evil that he had threatened to do to them; he did not carry it out.
—JONAH 3:10

My fate is not set in stone but lies in my willingness to repent and to cooperate with the loving will of God. It's never too late to turn away from any evil—great or small—and to turn my heart toward God.

Jonah 3:1–10
Psalm 51
Luke 11:29–32

Queen Esther, seized with mortal anguish had recourse to the LORD. . . .
"Now help me, who am alone and have no one but you, O LORD
my God."
—ESTHER C:12, 14

I love a queen with recourse! Esther, we note, in "mortal anguish"—that's an anguish so deep, it's deadly—turns to the Lord in recourse. That is, she turns to him for protection. But recourse can also indicate a kind of "right to make demands." Esther had recourse, the right to demand protection, precisely because she knew who she was talking to, precisely because she believed in God's unfailing protection for the orphan, the defenseless, the vulnerable, and the marginalized.

Esther C:12, 14–16, 23–25
Psalm 138
Matthew 7:7–12

FEBRUARY 22

"And so I say to you, you are Peter, and upon this rock I will build my Church, and the gates of the netherworld shall not prevail against it."
—MATTHEW 16:18

In recent years, as scandals have rippled throughout the Church, I've been reminded that the Church will not be brought down by television cameras or newspaper reports. We will outlast the latest newscast. I'm also reminded that I have a deep and penetrating responsibility to pray for Church leadership, for their wisdom, protection, strength, and courage to lead this motley flock.

Today, let's offer up our Lenten fasting for the pope.

1 Peter 5:1–4
Psalm 23
Matthew 16:13–19

Saturday

FEBRUARY 23

Blessed are they who observe his decrees,
who seek him with all their heart.
—PSALM 119:2

Moses says of the Ten Commandments, "be careful, then,
to observe them with all your heart and with all your soul."
It is not only a matter of observing the letter of the law; but
there is also a seeking with the whole heart that must
inform our every waking moment. This is a wholeness of
spirit that God intends for us, a blessedness that will
descend upon the spirit who not only keeps the law, but
also loves the law and the Lord who spoke it.

Deuteronomy 26:16–19
Psalm 119
Matthew 5:43–48

FEBRUARY 24

• SECOND SUNDAY OF LENT •

Then from the cloud came a voice that said, "This is my chosen Son;
listen to him."
—LUKE 9:35

Jesus was transfigured and dazzling, speaking to prophets
long dead, surrounded in a cloud from which a voice
proclaims, "This is my chosen Son; listen to him." It must
have been a terrifying mystery sometimes to be an apostle
of Jesus'. They usually didn't understand the significance of
the events they were a part of, and sometimes a voice had
to break through the cloud of mystery and state things very
plainly. Today, I cling to that simplicity and listen to Jesus.

Genesis 15:5–12, 17–18
Psalm 27
Philippians 3:17—4:1 or 3:20—4:1
Luke 9:28–36

FEBRUARY 25

Give and gifts will be given to you; a good measure, packed together,
shaken down, and overflowing, will be poured into your lap.
—LUKE 6:38

You've probably heard it said: you cannot out-give God. But
you are most welcome to try.

Daniel 9:4b–10
Psalm 79
Luke 6:36–38

Learn to do good.
—ISAIAH 1:17

There's Isaiah, always handing out the easy assignments. We might tease the "do-gooders" among us who are always taking up some cause, spending precious free time with the homeless, the orphan, the elderly, and the sick. We admire them—from a distance—but think *not me, I don't have the time, the energy, the resources to get involved.* If we didn't need guidance in learning to do good, the Church might not be so obvious with suggestions such as the corporal works of mercy.

Isaiah 1:10, 16–20
Psalm 50
Matthew 23:1–12

I hear the whispers of the crowd, that frighten me from every side,
as they consult together against me, plotting to take my life.
But my trust is in you, O, LORD:
I say, "You are my God."
—PSALM 31:14–15

Most of us will not experience plots against our lives; most of us will not experience martyrdom or life-threatening persecutions. But we'll probably know what it feels like to be falsely accused, misjudged, misunderstood, or outcast. To be faithful is to stand outside the whispering crowd. Let them whisper. Our trust is not in plotting and petty people, but in the Lord, Jesus Christ, who is Judge, Mighty Ruler, Sovereign King, and Savior.

Jeremiah 18:18–20
Psalm 31
Matthew 20:17–28

FEBRUARY 28

More tortuous than all else is the human heart,
beyond remedy; who can understand it?
I, the LORD, alone probe the mind
and test the heart,
To reward everyone according to his ways,
according to the merit of his deeds.
—JEREMIAH 17:9–10

God has given me a permanent reprieve from judging,
criticizing, or evaluating anyone. May I have the good
sense to take it.

Jeremiah 17:5–10
Psalm 1
Luke 16:19–31

They sold Joseph to the Ishmaelites for twenty pieces of silver.
—GENESIS 37:28

And we know what happened to him.

Family can be tough business, heart-breaking business that calls out of us a deeper capacity to forgive and love than we could ever conjure on our own. To do this at all, much less to do it well, we must lean on Jesus—in the sacraments, in prayer, in the intercession of saints and friends.

Even if my own family should forsake me, Lord, you do not forget your own. You rescue me from slavery and make me honorable in the eyes of my enemies.

Genesis 37:3–4, 12–13, 17–28
Psalm 105
Matthew 21:33–43, 45–46

MARCH 2

"A man had two sons . . ."
—LUKE 15:11

The story of the prodigal son is universally well-known because it touches on so much that is common to the human condition. Today, spend some time reading it and immersing yourself in the story. Imagine yourself in it, first as the prodigal son, then as the older brother, and finally as the father. Which is the hardest role to play, and what might that tell you about how you need to pray?

Micah 7:14–15, 18–20
Psalm 103
Luke 15:1–3, 11–32

MARCH 3

He pardons all your iniquities,
he heals all your ills,
He redeems your life from destruction,
he crowns you with kindness and compassion.
—PSALM 103:3–4

There is a rhythm and order here that we may want to pause and consider. Healing follows pardon; redemption follows healing; the rewards of redemption are kindness and compassion.

Exodus 3:1–8a, 13–15
Psalm 103
1 Corinthians 10:1–6, 10–12
Luke 13:1–9

Send forth your light and your fidelity;
they shall lead me on
and bring me to your holy mountain,
to your dwelling-place.
—PSALM 43:3

May I be led today, not by ego, self-will, fear, or selfishness, but by trust in your faithfulness and the light of your word.

2 Kings 5:1–15ab
Psalm 42, 43
Luke 4:24–30

MARCH 5

Unless each of you forgives your brother from your heart.
—MATTHEW 18:35

The consequences of unforgiveness are brutal. Could it possibly be worth it to carry resentment? Does anything good come from that?

"Seventy times seven." There's a reason I am so strongly warned about the tragedy of unforgiveness; Jesus wants to free *my* heart.

Daniel 3:25, 34–43
Psalm 25
Matthew 18:21–35

MARCH 6

Take care and be earnestly on your guard not to forget the things which your own eyes have seen, nor let them slip from your memory as long as you live, but teach them to your children and to your children's children.
—DEUTERONOMY 4:9

We sometimes attribute to St. Francis this maxim: Teach always, and when necessary, use words.

What lessons do my actions teach? Do I share what I know with an open heart? When asked, do I share my experience, faith, and hope with those who need it?

Deuteronomy 4:1, 5–9
Psalm 147
Matthew 5:17–19

*This is the nation that does not listen to the voice of the LORD, its God,
or take correction.*
—JEREMIAH 7:28

The results of not listening to God's voice are devastating:
hardened hearts, barrenness, isolation, and death.

Lord, give me a teachable spirit.

Jeremiah 7:23–28
Psalm 95
Luke 11:14–23

*There shall be no strange god among you
nor shall you worship any alien god.
I, the LORD, am your God
who led you forth from the land of Egypt.*
—PSALM 81:9–10

I would never admit to worshipping food or money or
status or a human being. But do these "aliens" occasionally
creep into the space that should be occupied solely by
God? What might be the best way to return them to their
proper sphere and to take up a proper worship of the One
who leads me out of the slavery that is sin?

Hosea 14:2–10
Psalm 81
Mark 12:28–34

MARCH 9

For it is love that I desire, not sacrifice,
and knowledge of God rather than burnt offerings.
—HOSEA 6:6

Going through the motions is not enough; actions void of meaning kill a relationship.

Lord, you want my heart, and I will not withhold it from you.

Hosea 6:1–6
Psalm 51
Luke 18:9–14

*Whoever is in Christ is a new creation: the old things have passed
away; behold, new things have come.*
—2 CORINTHIANS 5:17

How the prodigal son must have longed to take back some
of his choices. Who among us has not felt his regret and
sorrow? But the Father offers us something better than
going back in time. We're offered even more than
forgiveness; in reconciliation, we are made new. In Christ,
you are a new creation. New.

Joshua 5:9a, 10–12
Psalm 34
2 Corinthians 5:17–21
Luke 15:1–3, 11–32

Lo, I am about to create new heavens
and a new earth;
The things of the past shall not be remembered
or come to mind
Instead there shall always be rejoicing and happiness in what I create;
for I created Jerusalem to be a joy
and its people to be a delight.
—ISAIAH 65:17–19

God is up to something new in you. Look for delight today,
for joy and creativity and holy happiness.

Isaiah 65:17–21
Psalm 30
John 4:43–54

MARCH 12

Jesus said to him, "Rise, take up your mat, and walk." Immediately the
man became well, took up his mat, and walked.
—JOHN 5:8–9

My healing may be immediate or take place over time; my
ailments may be physical or spiritual or both. The point is
that Jesus is always interested in my coming to him with
every need, great and small; he is always interested in my
well-being.

Ezekiel 47:1–9, 12
Psalm 46
John 5:1–16

Can a mother forget her infant, / be without tenderness for the child of her womb? / Even should she forget, / I will never forget you.
—ISAIAH 49:15

The bond unveiled is a strong one, flesh and blood, a body begotten of another body. Always real, of the most essential, original, and intimate character. Never to be dissolved or diluted. Never to be severed. Indeed, the bond we share with God is essential and visceral, tender and eternal.

Isaiah 49:8–15
Psalm 145
John 5:17–30

MARCH 14

"I came in the name of my Father."
—JOHN 5:43

It was blasphemous for Jesus to refer to God as Father.
Implying such intimacy would have railed against the ears
of the Pharisees. Yet, our readings are intent upon
establishing familial relationships, blood ties: Jesus comes in
the name of the Father; we are sons and daughters of God.
Why might that be? What are the implications of these
blood ties for us, now?

Exodus 32:7–14
Psalm 106
John 5:31–47

MARCH 15

*So they tried to arrest him, but no one laid a hand upon him, because his
hour had not yet come.*
—JOHN 7:30

God has his timing, even in our struggles. I can trust that
even my suffering can be surrendered to eternal precision
for the holiest, most redemptive possible outcome.

Wisdom 2:1a, 12–22
Psalm 34
John 7:1–2, 10, 25–30

A shield before me is God,
who saves the upright of heart.
—PSALM 7:10

God will protect everything in me that is good and upright;
he will fan the flame of every good thing in me.

How am I being protected, shielded from evil? Where is
God blessing me and causing me to flourish?

Jeremiah 11:18–20
Psalm 7
John 7:40–53

⇒ 105 ⇐

MARCH 17

See, I am doing something new!
Now it springs forth, do you not perceive it?
In the desert I make a way,
in the wasteland, rivers.
—ISAIAH 43:19

In the desert places of our deepest being, a spring bubbles up. In the wasteland of our sin and obstinacy, living water moves.

Isaiah 43:16–21
Psalm 126
Philippians 3:8–14
John 8:1–11

Jesus spoke to them again, saying, "I am the light of the world. Whoever follows me will not walk in darkness, but will have the light of life."
—JOHN 8:12

I acknowledge the darkness of my ignorance, the darkness of my sin, the darkness of my selfishness, despair, or weakness. There are shadows cast in this fallen world, brutal black clouds hovering over the human horizon, stretched by our fears to the very ends of existence. Jesus, be our light.

Daniel 13:1–9, 15–17, 19–30, 33–62 or 13:41c–62
Psalm 23
John 8:12–20

When Joseph awoke, he did as the angel of the Lord had commanded
him and took his wife into his home.
—MATTHEW 1:24

There are saints who dazzle us and those who are hidden.
Pope Paul VI says it this way: "St. Joseph is the model of
those humble ones that Christianity raises up to great
destinies . . . he is the proof that in order to be a good and
genuine follower of Christ, there is no need of great
things—it is enough to have the common, simple and
human virtues, but they need to be true and authentic."

Jesus, make us authentic.

2 Samuel 7:4–5, 12–14, 16
Psalm 89:2–3, 4–5, 27, 29
Romans 4:13, 16–18, 22
Matthew 1:16, 18–21, 24a or Luke 2:41–51a

MARCH 20

I see four men unfettered and unhurt, walking in the fire, and the fourth looks like a son of God.
—DANIEL 3:25

As adventure stories go, the book of Daniel is as good as they come. Shadrach, Meshach, Abednego, and an angel sent from heaven walk through the fire meant to execute them and satisfy Nebuchadnezzer's fury. But there's no fiery pit that God's reach cannot penetrate for love of his own. And there is no greater adventure than to see God's hand at work in the lives of real people and in the angels who attend them.

Daniel 3:14–20, 91–92, 95
Daniel 3:52, 53, 54, 55, 56
John 8:31–42

MARCH 21

Jesus said to them, "Amen, amen, I say to you, before Abraham came to be, I AM."
—JOHN 8:58

Jesus is always drawing us out of time and into eternity.

For today, I will live my life believing in the fullness of eternal reality.

Genesis 17:3–9
Psalm 105
John 8:51–59

I love you, O LORD, my strength.
—PSALM 18:2

I know God doesn't need me. I know Jesus doesn't need to
hear me say that I love him. But the Psalms are so filled
with affection and praise, with simple adoration: I love you.
Would it hurt if I were just a bit more expressive with my
affection for God? Would it change anything—would it
change me—if I were to allow such tender sentiments to
rise to the surface more often?

Jeremiah 20:10–13
Psalm 18
John 10:31–42

I will turn their mourning into joy,
I will console and gladden them after their sorrows.
—JEREMIAH 31:13

It seems that there's always this link between sorrow and joy. There is a dynamic tension between the two that God uses to draw us to him, a mysterious link that reveals his hand in all. He can transform everything for our good; he makes a way where there is none; joy becomes sorrow all grown up.

Ezekiel 37:21–28
Jeremiah 31:10–13
John 11:45–56

MARCH 24

• PALM SUNDAY OF THE LORD'S PASSION •

He said to them, "I have eagerly desired to eat this Passover with you
before I suffer."
—LUKE 22:15

Jesus eagerly desires to give himself to us. When I receive
the Holy Eucharist, am I eager to give myself back?

Luke 19:28–40
Isaiah 50:4–7
Psalm 22
Philippians 2:6–11
Luke 22:14—23:56

Mary took a liter of costly perfumed oil made from genuine aromatic nard and anointed the feet of Jesus and dried them with her hair; the house was filled with the fragrance of the oil.
—JOHN 12:3

I see her: on hands and knees, robes dragging in the dust. Humble, unworthy to anoint the head of Jesus, she hovers over his feet. The room is thick with the aroma of her affection and tenderness. Pride, greed, and selfishness cannot overcome it.

Isaiah 42:1–7
Psalm 27
John 12:1–11

MARCH 26

"The cock will not crow before you deny me three times."
—JOHN 13:38

The one who loves Jesus so much, who boldly proclaims, "I will lay down my life for you," denies him and flees. Peter's story is captured, not just as an accurate account of events, but to remind me that Jesus goes to the cross with full knowledge of my defeat and weakness, my failures and betrayals. It is for my sin that he enters into his Passion. It is with great, tender love for me that he walks to Calvary.

Isaiah 49:1–6
Psalm 71
John 13:21–33, 36–38

MARCH 27

I have not rebelled,
have not turned back.
I gave my back to those who beat me,
my cheeks to those who plucked my beard;
My face I did not shield
from buffets and spitting.
—ISAIAH 50:5–6

This writer is supple in God's hands, willing to go wherever he is led and to endure much for God's greater glory. How I resist my sufferings and fight God's work in me. Jesus, teach me not to resist the hand that guides me through suffering to redemption, through darkness and sin to radiant love and a luminous, eternal freedom.

Isaiah 50:4–9
Psalm 69
Matthew 26:14–25

MARCH 28

• HOLY THURSDAY •

Jesus knew that his hour had come to pass from this world to the Father.
He loved his own in the world and he loved them to the end.
—JOHN 13:1

The road home to the Father was dark indeed. Jesus loves
to the end by serving to the end, by giving himself
completely. And what comes to pass? In the end, even in
this world, his love reigns.

Chrism Mass:
Isaiah 61:1–3a, 6a, 8–9
Psalm 89
Revelation 1:5–8
Luke 4:16–21

Evening Mass of the Lord's Supper:
Exodus 12:1–8, 11–14
Psalm 116
1 Corinthians 11:23–26
John 13:1–15

Yet it was our infirmities that he bore,
our sufferings that he endured,
while we thought of him as stricken,
as one smitten by God and afflicted.
But he was pierced for our offenses,
crushed for our sins;
upon him was the chastisement that makes us whole,
by his stripes we were healed.
—ISAIAH 53:4–5

We venerate the cross and kneel in silence—the Church remembering the reality of all that is accomplished on the cross. May a part of my heart always be kneeling.

Isaiah 52:13—53:12
Psalm 31
Hebrews 4:14–16; 5:7–9
John 18:1—19:42

For a brief moment I abandoned you,
But with great tenderness I will take you back.
—ISAIAH 54:7

God is not tempestuous. The great sweep of the Vigil readings marks our history and reminds us that we are part of a much larger story, an eternal story, in which God takes us back again and again in great tenderness.

Vigil:
Genesis 1:1—2:2 or 1:1, 26–31
Psalm 104 or 33
Genesis 22:1–18 or 22:1–2, 9–13, 15–18
Psalm 16
Exodus 14:15—15:1
Exodus 15:1–6, 17–18
Isaiah 54:5–14

Psalm 30
Isaiah 55:1–11
Isaiah 12:2–6
Baruch 3:9–15, 32—4:4
Psalm 19
Ezekiel 36:16–28
Romans 6:3–11
Psalm 118
Luke 24:1–12

MARCH 31

On the first day of the week, Mary of Magdala came to the tomb early in the morning, while it was still dark, and saw the stone removed from the tomb.
—JOHN 20:1

She was the first to the tomb, anonymous and insignificant in the world's eyes. In her mourning, she sought you in the dark unknowing. Lord, let me be eager to seek you early in the morning, in the dawn of my faith. Let me discover the stone rolled away. Though the world may not see me at all, may I enter the mystery of your Resurrection, where you call me by name.

Acts 10:34a, 37–43
Psalm 118
1 Corinthians 5:6–8 or Colossians 3:1–4
John 20:1–9 or Luke 24:1–12 or Luke 24:13–35

APRIL 1

You will show me the path to life,
fullness of joys in your presence,
the delights at your right hand forever.
—PSALM 16:11

You can spot a promise of heaven because it has eternal
hues: life, fullness, and holy delight.

Acts 2:14, 22–33
Psalm 16
Matthew 28:8–15

Tuesday

APRIL 2

• ST. FRANCIS OF PAOLA, HERMIT •

"Rabbouni!"
—JOHN 20:16

Recognition pours over her like a healing balm. Such sweet relief on finding the one she seeks. There is such tenderness in the moment when all that we have lost—and more—is restored to us.

Rabbouni—Teacher—let us seek you and find you.

Acts 2:36–41
Psalm 33
John 20:11–18

He was made known to them in the breaking of the bread.
—LUKE 24:35

The Eucharist is a constant and living revelation of Jesus.
Go to Mass expectant, hoping in revelation.

Acts 3:1–10
Psalm 105
Luke 24:13–35

APRIL 4

• ST. ISIDORE, BISHOP AND DOCTOR OF THE CHURCH •

He stood in their midst and said to them, "Peace be with you."
—LUKE 24:36

He stands in our midst—in adoration, in the Mass and the
sacraments, in Scripture, in our meditations and prayers and
longings, in myriad ways—speaking into our most hopeless
tumult, "Peace."

Acts 3:11–26
Psalm 8
Luke 24:35–48

⇒ 124 ⇐

Friday

APRIL 5

• ST. VINCENT FERRER, PRIEST •

O LORD, grant prosperity!
—PSALM 118:25

Prosperity: the condition of being successful or thriving;
well-being.

Prosperous: flourishing.

Grant: to bestow or transfer formally.

Acts 4:1–12
Psalm 118
John 21:1–14

"Go into the whole world and proclaim the Gospel to every creature."
—MARK 16:15

"Grace," writes Hans Urs von Balthasar, "brings man a task, opens up for him a field of activity, bestows upon him the joy of accomplishment, so that he can identify himself with his mission and discover in it the true meaning of his existence. Grace gives man a center of gravity . . . For man's mission in life is not something general and impersonal like a ready-made coat; it has been designed specifically for him and given into his possession as the most personal of all gifts. By it he becomes, in the fullest sense of the word, a person."

Acts 4:13–21
Psalm 118
Mark 16:9–15

Many signs and wonders were done among the people at the hands of the apostles . . . Yet more than ever, believers in the Lord, great numbers of men and women, were added to them.
—ACTS 5:12, 16

Is my life a living sign? Do I speak, love, and live in such a way that others are invited into the great number of believers? Is the Truth active and attractive in me?

Acts 5:12–16
Psalm 118
Revelation 1:9–11a, 12–13, 17–19
John 20:19–31

To do your will, O God, is my delight,
and your law is within my heart!
—PSALM 40:8

There is something natural about God's law; it is written
across our natural hearts. We are meant for it and will find
our flourishing within it. The law does not deaden us but
brings us alive to live as we were meant to. It is not imposed
upon us but already dwells within us. When we fight
against this law that's written into our person, strife and
inner turmoil get the upper hand.

Isaiah 7:10–14; 8:10
Psalm 40
Hebrews 10:4–10
Luke 1:26–38

APRIL 9

The community of believers was of one heart and mind.
—ACTS 4:32

I doubt that the community of believers has been so united
since it first developed in Jerusalem. Still, unity is the goal:
communion with our brethren, drawing those who struggle
in their belief into the heart and mind of the Church. We
do this by being simple, clear, gentle, and direct. But above
all, by loving.

Acts 4:32–37
Psalm 93
John 3:7b–15

APRIL 10

Look to him that you may be radiant with joy.
—PSALM 34:5

Thomas Merton said it this way: "We have a wonderful vocation. Christ has brought us here to live, to live and breathe and be happy under his gaze, to play in his sight like children, while he takes care of us."

Acts 5:17–26
Psalm 34
John 3:16–21

The Father loves the Son and has given everything over to him.
—JOHN 3:35

In love you have been entrusted to the hands of a master carpenter. May he build you up from an ageless foundation, walls ever reaching toward heaven, a holy shelter for the Spirit of God.

Acts 5:27–33
Psalm 34
John 3:31–36

*That I may gaze on the loveliness of the LORD
and contemplate his temple.*
—PSALM 27:4

When Blessed John Paul II visited Spain in 2003, he told
the youth gathered before him, "The drama of
contemporary culture is the lack of interiority, the absence
of contemplation. . . . When the contemplative spirit is
missing, life is not protected and all that is human is
denigrated. Without interiority, modern man puts his own
integrity at risk."

To gaze on God's loveliness is not simply an act of worship,
but an act of integration.

Acts 5:34–42
Psalm 27
John 6:1–15

"Brothers, select from among you seven reputable men, filled with the Spirit and wisdom, whom we shall appoint to this task, whereas we shall devote ourselves to prayer and to the ministry of the word" . . . They presented these men to the Apostles who prayed and laid hands on them.
—ACTS 6:3–6

Promise yourself you will attend an ordination this spring, to see people ordained either to be deacons or priests. Study the rites so that you're educated and open to what is happening.

Acts 6:1–7
Psalm 33
John 6:16–21

"It is the Lord."
—JOHN 21:7

The apostles didn't recognize Jesus even when he was standing plainly before them. And sometimes, neither do I.

Lord, sometimes I don't recognize your presence, though you stand before me, guiding me toward an ever more abundant, hopeful life of purpose and import. Help me, Jesus, to see you, to know your voice, and to follow where you lead.

Acts 5:27–32, 40b–41
Psalm 30
Revelation 5:11–14
John 21:1–19 or 21:1–14

Do not work for food that perishes but for the food that endures for eternal life.
—JOHN 6:27

I like food. I like material comforts—a soft bed, a car that runs, money in the bank. Is Jesus asking me to give up all passing things?

God knows my need. And, living in reality, I must encounter material goods and riches and even superfluous comforts. Perhaps it is better to ask, how tight is my grasp on these things? Is my life ordered only toward material riches, or do I save and cultivate precious space for heaven in every day?

Acts 6:8–15
Psalm 119
John 6:22–29

APRIL 16

"Lord, do not hold this sin against them."
—ACTS 7:60

This prayer was found in the Ravensbrück concentration camp near the body of a dead child: "O Lord, remember not only men and women of good will, but also those of ill will. But do not remember all the suffering they inflicted on us. Remember the fruits we have born thanks to this suffering: our comradeship, our humility, our courage, our generosity, the greatness of heart which has grown out of this; and when they come to judgment let all the fruits that we have born be their forgiveness."

Acts 7:51—8:1a
Psalm 31
John 6:30–35

For unclean spirits, crying out in a loud voice, came out of many possessed people, and many paralyzed and crippled people were cured. There was great joy in that city.
—ACTS 8:7–8

First there is strife and resistance. There is the loud cry, the tumult and lament and pain of the healing work. But then, great joy comes—and stays.

Acts 8:1b–8
Psalm 66
John 6:35–40

⇒ 137 ⇐

APRIL 18

"I am the living bread that came down from heaven; whoever eats this bread will live forever; and the bread that I will give is my Flesh for the life of the world."
—JOHN 6:51

Pope Leo XIII wrote, "We become what we receive." Maybe I could pay more attention to what I let pass over the transom of my self.

Acts 8:26–40
Psalm 66
John 6:44–51

Immediately, things like scales fell from his eyes and he regained his sight.
—ACTS 9:18

Why in the world would God choose the persecuting Saul as an instrument for God's work? Maybe to remind us that grace can do anything, accomplish anything, restore anyone, and convert even our worst enemy—the one bent on our torture and persecution—to become our most faithful and right-sighted advocate.

Acts 9:1–20
Psalm 117:1–2
John 6:52–59

You have loosed my bonds.
—PSALM 116:16

Where am I powerless? What keeps me bound? Do I believe that God can free me from these chains—from any addiction or sin? From all fear? What keeps me from entrusting the most enslaved part of myself to his care?

Please note that this passage is in the past tense. The work in you, this loosing, is already accomplished in heaven.

Acts 9:31–42
Psalm 116
John 6:60–69

My sheep hear my voice; I know them, and they follow me. I give them eternal life, and they shall never perish. No one can take them out of my hand.
—JOHN 10:27–28

This is no mere gentle reassurance meant for some distant pondering. Jesus invites us to embrace a radical sense of security and confidence meant to bolster us as we move through the world in the best interests of the Gospel, in the best interests of eternal love.

Acts 13:14, 43–52
Psalm 100
Revelation 7:9, 14b–17
John 10:27–30

Athirst is my soul for God, the living God.
When shall I go and behold the face of God?
—PSALM 42:2

The woman in front of me in church holds a chubby
toddler who is preoccupied with her mother's face, as so
many young ones are. With her child's hands, she keeps
drawing her mother's face to hers. Wide-eyed and open, she
gazes at her mother's face with endless fascination,
dissatisfied with anything less than eye-to-eye connection,
the intensity of childlike wonder and adulation.

Acts 11:1–18
Psalm 42
John 10:1–10

My sheep hear my voice; I know them, and they follow me.
—JOHN 10:27

I used to find the shepherd-sheep metaphor a little too "husbandry." Then I read an article that noted that sheep were easily terrified, prone to wander off, and needed constant attention and protection from predators. It was not uncommon to combine herds at night in communal pens and separate them the following day. This separation was accomplished simply by the shepherd calling to the sheep. The sheep knew the voice that well. They knew that the voice meant security, care, attention, protection, and when necessary, rescue.

Acts 11:19–26
Psalm 87
John 10:22–30

"I came into the world as light, so that everyone who believes in me might not remain in darkness."
—JOHN 12:46

When I lived in Alaska, my favorite time of year was spring; we gained seven minutes of sunlight every day. Spring was not a quiet creeping season so much as a wild explosion of light breaking out over the frozen earth—dazzling and brilliant, living energy that meant warmth and growth and green things. Though it might like to linger, the darkness of the long winter months was forced to give way to light.

Christ must love spring on the tundra.

Acts 12:24–13:5
Psalm 67
John 12:44–50

APRIL 25

The heavens proclaim your wonders, O LORD.
—PSALM 89:5

When I was little, I wanted to be an astronaut. When I got
to college, I dropped Astronomy 101 on the second day of
class. Physics! So I write instead. But I still look to the
heavens. I still stammer in wonder at the vast worlds
hovering above us. I still understand right down to my
bones why the psalmist chooses again and again to draw
our gaze upward and out, beyond the walls of this world.

1 Peter 5:5b–14
Psalm 89
Mark 16:15–20

Do not let your hearts be troubled. You have faith in God; have faith
also in me. In my Father's house there are many dwelling places. . . .
And if I go and prepare a place for you, I will come back again and take
you to myself so that where I am you also may be.
—JOHN 14:1–3

Sheep are easily terrified, and too often, so am I. One of my greatest fears is being left behind, abandoned, as though Jesus will take everyone but me with him to heaven. It is a common fear, if immature. It disbelieves the very heart of the Gospel message: "I will come back again and take you to myself so that where I am you also may be."

Acts 13:26–33
Psalm 2
John 14:1–6

And whatever you ask in my name, I will do, so that the Father may be glorified in the Son. If you ask anything of me in my name, I will do it.
—JOHN 14:13–14

Jesus doesn't lie, so how can this promise in John's Gospel be true? What do we do with the conundrum of prayers that seem to go unanswered or where the answer is no? It is pure vanity to imagine that my prayers are perfect, not riddled with impure motives of every variety. My own sin is likely the most obvious obstacle to the effectiveness of grace.

Acts 13:44–52
Psalm 98
John 14:7–14

APRIL 28

• FIFTH SUNDAY OF EASTER •

"I give you a new commandment: love one another. This is how all will know that you are my disciples, if you have love for one another."
—JOHN 13:34–35

Loving another means desiring and delighting in that person's good, but how can I know what another's good is? This isn't easy, and it isn't always our job. But God has not left me to my own devices. I draw from the Church's wisdom, her saints and the sacraments, from trusted brethren and spiritual directors, from prayer and meditation with God's word. The Lord never gives us a commandment that we cannot follow or figure out.

Acts 14:21–27
Psalm 145
Revelation 21:1–5a
John 13:31–33a, 34–35

APRIL 29

• ST. CATHERINE OF SIENA, VIRGIN AND DOCTOR OF THE CHURCH •

"Whoever loves me, he will keep my word; and my Father will love him,
and we will come to him and make our dwelling with him."
—JOHN 14:23

St. Catherine of Siena would often tell those who came to
her for help: "Build an inner cell in your soul and never
leave it." The Lord frequently spoke to her in visions of this
notion: "My daughter, think always of Me, and I promise to
think of you." "Empty your heart of all other cares and
thoughts, think only of life and rest in Me. And be assured
that I think of you, I who can and will provide you richly
with everything you need."

Acts 14:5–18
Psalm 115:1–2, 3–4, 15–16
John 14:21–26

Do not let your hearts be troubled or afraid.
—JOHN 14:27

Implied here is our ability to surrender to fear; we can consciously participate in fear's terrible cascade within the human person. Implied here is the possibility of making a different choice, to turn away from fear, to chase it down and shackle it, disarm it before it takes over. "Do not allow fear to overtake you," indeed, "Do let your hearts be overtaken by love."

Lord, take dominion in my heart.

Acts 14:19–28
Psalm 145
John 14:27–31

Whatever you do, do from the heart, as for the Lord and not for me, knowing that you will receive from the Lord the due payment of the inheritance; be slaves of the Lord Christ.
—COLOSSIANS 3:23–24

From the time I was a child, I have prayed to St. Joseph the Worker. I'm not wealthy, but my life is rich. Work has never been perfect, but it's always interesting, and I have never been truly disappointed. As the years pass, my work becomes more rooted in my spiritual gifts; my office now hovers directly above an altar where Mass is celebrated nearly every day.

Thank you, St. Joseph, for your unfailing intercession.

Genesis 1:26–2:3 or Colossians 3:14–15, 17, 23–24
Psalm 90
Matthew 13:54–58

Commit to the LORD your way;
trust in him, and he will act.
—PSALM 37:5

Before you even uttered your prayer, he was acting. He is
acting, even now.

1 John 5:1–5
Psalm 37
Matthew 10:22–25

Friday

MAY 3

Philip said to him, "Master, show us the Father, and that will be enough for us." Jesus said to him, "Have I been with you for so long a time and you still do not know me, Philip?"
—JOHN 14:8–9

The saints encourage us, not only in holiness but also in the steady path to holiness. Philip here reminds us that it takes a long while for some of us to see with the heart, to convert the mind, to come to understand how the truth is ever before us.

Pray for us, St. Philip and St. James, that we may come to know Jesus and to love him.

1 Corinthians 15:1–8
Psalm 19
John 14:6–14

MAY 4

If the world hates you, realize that it hated me first. If you belonged to the world, the world would love its own; but because you do not belong to the world, and I have chosen you out of the world, the world hates you.
—JOHN 15:18–19

Diets, debt, economic trends, fashion statements, bank statements, political strife, natural disasters, disastrous health, disastrous relationships, worrying what other people think, every shade of fear and sin and self-serving: these things do not own you. You belong to another; your heart came from and is returning to another world where thin, rich, popular, successful, or healthy no longer resounds as the most worthy thing you could be.

Acts 16:1–10
Psalm 100
John 15:18–21

Sunday

MAY 5

• SIXTH SUNDAY OF EASTER •

The city had no need of sun or moon to shine on it, for the glory of God gave it light, and its lamp was the Lamb.
—REVELATION 21:22–23

Jesus is the source. He is the way, the truth, and the life—*our* light, our salvation, and our hope. Every prayer is answered, every hope fulfilled, every holy promise kept in the Lamb.

Acts 15:1–2, 22–29
Psalm 67
Revelation 21:10–14, 22–23
John 14:23–29

Monday

MAY 6

The Lord opened her heart to pay attention.
—ACTS 16:14

A simple woman, sitting simply in prayer. God does his part. This passage should give us great confidence and courage that the Lord will help us—to understand, to find our way, to find love and let love find us, to trust and hope, to believe, to love well. He will come and find us in prayer. And he will open our hearts to know him, love him, and serve him.

Acts 16:11–15
Psalm 149
John 15:26—16:4a

Tuesday

MAY 7

In the presence of angels, I will sing your praise.
—PSALM 138:1

Indeed, there's very little one can do that is not in the
presence of angels.

Acts 16:22–34
Psalm 138
John 16:5–11

Jesus said to his disciples . . . "when he comes, the Spirit of truth, he will guide you to all truth."
—JOHN 16:12, 13

Falling in love with the truth is exactly like falling in love with a person; it ebbs and flows, grows deeper, richer, and more real over time. Some of us experience it like being struck by lightning and others more like floating down a river with its combination of calm water and rapids. But when the Spirit is with us, we are drawn more deeply into the truth of Jesus. The Spirit continues to fan the flame Jesus ignited at the moment of our conversion.

Acts 17:15 22—18:1
Psalm 148
John 16:12–15

As he blessed them he parted from them and was taken up to heaven.
—LUKE 24:51

After such a humble and hidden entrance into the
world—with shepherds and stable and dark of night—why
the dramatic exit? God will go to any length to help us
perceive his presence with us. We might gripe at times
about wishing God was more obvious with us, but Scripture
makes clear that Jesus was the Messiah. His unexpected
entrance and dramatic exit are not because God needs to
grandstand, but because he is present and knows us
so well.

Acts 1:1–11
Psalm 47
Hebrews 9:24–28; 10:19–23 or Ephesians 1:17–23
Luke 24:46–53

Friday

MAY 10

• ST. DAMIEN JOSEPH DE VEUSTER, PRIEST •

*But I will see you again, and your hearts will rejoice, and no one will
take your joy away from you.*
—JOHN 16:22

"Joy," writes Peter Kreeft, "comes not from the world . . . or
from ourselves . . . but from God, through the spirit, it
'smells of divinity." Yes, and eternity."

Acts 18:9–18
Psalm 47
John 16:20–23

MAY 11

God sits upon his holy throne.
—PSALM 47:8

Which means I don't have to. I don't have to sit in judgment. I don't have to take on problems that are not mine. I'm not in charge, not in control of the universe—but someone is, someone who loves me and knows me by name. And this gives me confidence and courage to move through the world as a light, trusting that the eyes of God never leave me, even as he never leaves his holy throne.

Acts 18:23–28
Psalm 47
John 16:23–28

"Come, Lord Jesus!"
—REVELATION 22:20

These are virtually the last words of the Bible, and how
aptly they punctuate all that has come before it. "Come,
Lord Jesus!" must become my prayer, my posture, my desire,
my breath—my life. "Come, Lord Jesus!" can keep me
company in the direst need, the darkest loneliness, the
deepest sin and suffering. May it frequently be upon my
lips and always in my heart: "Come, Lord Jesus!"

Acts 7:55–60
Psalm 97
Revelation 22:12–14, 16–17, 20
John 17:20–26

In the world you will have trouble, but take courage, I have conquered the world.
—JOHN 16:33

I was fourteen years old when Pope John Paul II was shot. I remember it well—a gunman opening fire in St. Peter's Square. The pope frequently credited his survival and recovery to the intercession of Our Lady of Fatima. But the thing I remember most is the picture of John Paul taken later, seated with and leaning in toward the man who shot him. This is one who understands the meaning of Christian courage. Mercy and forgiveness conquer the world.

Acts 19:1–8
Psalm 68
John 16:29–33

*It was not you who chose me, but I who chose you and appointed you
to go and bear fruit that will remain.*
—JOHN 15:16

Carlo Carretto writes, "It is not I who wanted prayer. It is
he who wanted it. It is not I who have looked for him. It is
he who has looked for me first. . . . The hope on which my
prayer rests is in the fact that it is he who wants it. And if I
go to keep the appointment it is because he is already there
waiting for me."

Acts 1:15–17, 20–26
Psalm 113
John 15:9–17

Lifting up his eyes to heaven, Jesus prayed . . . "Holy Father, keep them in your name that you have given me, so that they may be one just as we are one."
—JOHN 17:9–11

Unity, communion, spiritual oneness: Jesus is always calling on the mystery of his complete union with the Father to teach us this unity. He gives us himself in the Eucharist to be a living example of this unity and sacrifice—maintaining his distinct person and yet being one with the Father. This spiritual union is not the shedding of our personhood, but paradoxically the fulfillment of it. Jesus and his Father are one, yet distinct.

Acts 20:28–38
Psalm 68
John 17:11b–19

And I have given them the glory you gave me, so that they may be one, as we are one, I in them and you in me, that they may be brought to perfection as one.
—JOHN 17:22–23

I am not my own private affair. My perfection cannot be achieved in isolation. Virtue grows only in communion. As the French Jesuit Jean Pierre de Caussade writes, "Do we not know that by all creatures and by every event the divine love desires to unite us to Himself, that He has ordained, arranged, or permitted everything about us, everything that happens to us with a view to this union?"

Acts 22:30; 23:6–11
Psalm 16
John 17:20–26

He said to him the third time, "Simon, son of John, do you love me?"
Peter was distressed that he had said to him a third time, "Do you love
me?" and he said to him, "Lord, you know everything; you know that I
love you." Jesus said to him, "Feed my sheep."
—JOHN 21:17

Did Jesus doubt Simon Peter's love? It's far more likely that
Peter doubted himself. Jesus was offering Peter a chance to
confess his love for him three times, where before Peter had
denied him three times. Jesus is always giving us
opportunities to rewrite our previous failings.

Acts 25:13b–21
Psalm 103
John 21:15–19

The upright shall see his face.
—PSALM 11:7

Every human longing is really directed toward this end: to
see your face, O Lord. The desire is so strong that at times I
think my heart will break. Receive my longing heart, Jesus.
Do not let this desire grow dim with the struggle to walk
with you. Do not allow me to reduce or diminish this
longing with things that do not satisfy; instead let me live
with my longing, until I am worthy to stand with you
face-to-face.

Acts 28:16–20, 30–31
Psalm 11
John 21:20–25

MAY 19

• PENTECOST SUNDAY •

"I will ask the Father, and he will give you another Advocate to be with you always."
—JOHN 14:16

Jesus was the Messiah the apostles had waited for their entire lives. Who was this Advocate he spoke of? Was Jesus abandoning them? The apostles' life of faith was constantly unfolding, moving toward deeper understanding—as ours is. May we know the presence of the Advocate, today and always.

Vigil:
Genesis 11:1–9 or Exodus 19:3–8, 16–20 or
Ezekiel 37:1–14 or Joel 3:1–5
Psalm 104
Romans 8:22–27
John 7:37–39
Extended Vigil:
Genesis 11:1–9
Psalm 33
Exodus 19:3–8a, 16–20b
Daniel 3:52–56
Ezekiel 37:1–14

Psalm 107
Joel 3:1–5
Psalm 104 or Psalm 33 or Daniel 3:52–56 or
Psalm 107
Romans 8:22–27
John 7:37–39
Day:
Acts 2:1–11
Psalm 104
1 Corinthians 12:3b–7, 12–13 or Romans 8:8–17
John 20:19–23 or John 14:15–16, 23–26

All wisdom comes from the LORD
and with him it remains forever, and is before all time.
—SIRACH 1:1

Wisdom is a gift from the Holy Spirit. We might be able to gather up knowledge for ourselves, but wisdom, in the theological sense—the ability to judge divine things—is pure gift. This is why Solomon prays for wisdom. This is why the divine gift of wisdom results in greater and more perfect love for God.

Sirach 1:1–10
Psalm 93
Mark 9:14–29

MAY 21

Accept whatever befalls you,
when sorrowful, be steadfast,
and in crushing misfortune be patient;
For in fire gold and silver are tested,
and worthy people in the crucible of humiliation.
—SIRACH 2:4–5

Jean Pierre de Caussade writes, "Everything arranged by God as regards actions and sufferings must be accepted with simplicity for those things that happen at each moment by the divine command or permission are always the most holy, the best and the most divine for us." Do you believe it? If you did, how would your day change?

Sirach 2:1–11
Psalm 37
Mark 9:30–37

Wisdom breathes life into her children.
—SIRACH 4:11

A singer knows that how you breathe is everything. A shallow breath might be interesting, used for dramatic effect. But a long, deep breath fills your whole body with the strength for sound that can soar or soften, rise or fall, resonate or whisper. A long, deep, well-formed breath makes you so much more in control, gives you so many more options for expression, is so much more full of life.

Sirach 4:11–19
Psalm 119
Mark 9:38–40

MAY 23

*Rely not on your own strength
in following the desires of your heart.*
—SIRACH 5:2

You can trust God with this thing you most desire. What is
it? A child, a home, a great love, someone who understands
you? Health for you or for another? Restoration of a lost
relationship, forgiveness from the one you hurt the most?
   You can trust God with this. He will hear you; he will
advocate for you; he will remove any obstacle to draw you
into the desires he formed within you

Sirach 5:1–8
Psalm 1
Mark 9:41–50

A faithful friend is a sturdy shelter;
he who finds one finds a treasure.
A faithful friend is beyond price,
no sum can balance his worth.
A faithful friend is a life-saving remedy,
such as he who fears God finds;
For he who fears God behaves accordingly,
and his friend will be like himself.
—SIRACH 6:14–17

Does this describe me? Am I a sturdy shelter, a life-saving remedy? Do I draw my friends closer to Jesus?

Sirach 6:5–17
Psalm 119
Mark 10:1–12

All their actions are clear as the sun to him,
his eyes are ever upon their ways.
—SIRACH 17:15

Nothing is hidden or confusing to God. It is a great comfort that Jesus knows me better than I know myself, especially when I do the thing I do not want to do, or struggle with certain recurrent sins, or fail to love and to live well. I can come before the Lord completely open and honest. Christ in his mercy brings me into greater understanding of myself by increasing my knowledge of his mercy and grace.

Sirach 17:1–15
Psalm 103
Mark 10:13–16

*We even boast of our affliction, knowing that affliction produces
endurance, and endurance, proven character, and proven character, hope
and hope does not disappoint, because the love of God has been poured
out into our hearts through the Holy Spirit that has been given to us.*
—ROMANS 5:3–5

Are you disappointed with your life, your work, your
relationships, your place in the world? Disappointment can
be as deadening to us as sin is. We are tempted to despair.
Disappointment believes in the world, but hope decides in
favor of God's logic and eternal reality. In God's logic,
"suffering . . . does not lead us away from God but toward
God," toward reality and hope.

Proverbs 8:22–31
Psalm 8
Romans 5:1–5
John 16:12–15

To the penitent God provides a way back,
he encourages those who are losing hope
and has chosen for them the lot of truth.
—SIRACH 17:24

Thomas Merton writes, "His eyes, which are the eyes of Truth, are fixed upon my heart. Where His glance falls, there is peace; for the light of His Face, which is the Truth, produces truth wherever it shines. . . . No grace comes to us from heaven except He looks upon our hearts." Today, dear Jesus, provide a way back; look upon my heart.

Sirach 17:20–24
Psalm 32
Mark 10:17–27

Tuesday

MAY 28

Give to the Most High as he has given to you,
generously, according to your means.

For the LORD is one who always repays,
and he will give back to you sevenfold.
—SIRACH 35:11

A single woman once told me that she believed her single
life was meant in part to serve as witness to those without
witnesses; "the world needs an audience." She is a popular
international lecturer. Her audience, worldwide—we might
say is "sevenfold." "According to your means" may mean
your time, your listening ear, or your ability to tell others
you see and hear them and acknowledge the simple
goodness of their existence.

Sirach 35:1–12
Psalm 50
Mark 10:28–31

⇒ 178 ⇐

Jesus said to them, "You do not know what you are asking. Can you drink the chalice that I drink or be baptized with the baptism with which I am baptized?" They said to him, "We can."
—MARK 10:38–39

Blessed John Henry Newman writes in his sermon "The Ventures of Faith," "Generous hearts, like James and John, or Peter, often speak largely and confidently beforehand of what they will do for Christ, not insincerely, yet ignorantly; and for their sincerity's sake they are taken at their word as a reward, though they have yet to learn how serious that word is. They say unto Him, 'We are able'—and the vow is recorded in heaven. This is the case of all of us at many seasons."

Sirach 36:1, 4–5a, 10–17
Psalm 79
Mark 10:32–45

MAY 30

"Master, I want to see."
—MARK 10:51

The request is bold and telling. The blind man knows what he is asking; more importantly, he knows who he is asking for healing.

Lord, today I do not forget who I am asking for healing and mercy.

Sirach 42:15–25
Psalm 33
Mark 10:46–52

Friday

MAY 31

• THE VISITATION OF THE BLESSED VIRGIN MARY •

"Blessed are you who believed that what was spoken to you by the Lord
would be fulfilled."
—LUKE 1:45

Blessed Mother, bring Jesus to me, too.

Zephaniah 3:14–18 or Romans 12:9–16
Isaiah 12:2–3, 4bcd, 5–6
Luke 1:39–56

JUNE 1

• ST. JUSTIN, MARTYR •

The precepts of the LORD are right,
rejoicing the heart.
—PSALM 19:9

Theologians teach us that the "supreme precept" of God is to love him with your whole heart and that there is no limit placed on this precept. In other words, there exists an endless depth in our capacity to love God—and therefore, an endlessness, an infinity of delight for the heart in love with God. The Lord's precepts are meant to increase and enflame eternal, delightful love.

Sirach 51:12cd–20
Psalm 19
Mark 11:27–33

JUNE 2

"Do this in remembrance of me."
—1 CORINTHIANS 11:24

When I was younger, I could not have articulated the teaching of transubstantiation; but when I came back to the Church it was for precisely this reason—I missed the Eucharist. I missed it deep in my bones, though I would not have been able to explain why. Body, mind, and spirit: though I might have wished to forget, no part of me could.

The Body and Blood of Christ changes us forever.

Lord, never let us take for granted your Presence.

Genesis 14:18–20
Psalm 110
1 Corinthians 11:23–26
Luke 9:11b–17

And I wept. Then at sunset I went out, dug a grave, and buried him.
—TOBIT 2:6–7

Tobit was moved by the loss of his kinsman, who was murdered in the marketplace. He mourns for him, and then does what is right and fitting, burying him after the sun went down on the Sabbath day. Something about the importance of burying the dead, showing honor to the body of the deceased, reminds us of the honor we must show to all the living.

Tobit 1:3—2:1a–8
Psalm 112
Mark 12:1–12

Blessed the man who fears the LORD.
—PSALM 112:1

In the Psalms, "fear of the Lord" is almost always another way of saying "reverence" or "worship." The opposite might be mockery or contempt. This can take many forms, some more subtle than others. We cannot have an intimate experience of reverence or worship without an intimate experience of the saving power of God. If we struggle to "fear" the Lord, we might ask ourselves, how has God saved me?

Tobit 2:9–14
Psalm 112
Mark 12:13–17

At that very time, the prayer of these two suppliants was heard in the glorious presence of Almighty God. So Raphael was sent to heal them both.
—TOBIT 3:16

I was praying about a difficult problem while on retreat and looked up just at the moment of my greatest lament to see a double rainbow stretched out across the lake, like a frame around my prayer. It lingered an unusually long while. God hears our prayers. Every little, lowly human utterance of my heart is heard by Almighty God. Though I may not recognize or understand the answer, he hears me and sends angels to heal me.

Tobit 3:1–11, 16–17
Psalm 25
Mark 12:18–27

"You shall love the Lord your God with all your heart, with all your soul, with all your mind and with all your strength." The second is this: "You shall love your neighbor as yourself." There is no other commandment greater than these.

Mark 12:29–30

Love is at the center of the answer to every question: loving well, loving completely, loving without condition. Whenever I might wonder what the right thing to do is, I can always find the answer in examining what, whom, and how I am loving.

Tobit 6:10–11; 7:1, 9–17; 8:4–9a
Psalm 128
Mark 12:28–34

I myself will pasture my sheep; I myself will give them rest, says the Lord God. The lost I will seek out, the strayed I will bring back, the injured I will bind up, the sick I will heal.
—EZEKIEL 34:15–16

This is the work of the Sacred Heart: to provide safety, rest, and restoration. The sacred heart of Jesus binds us, heals us, and brings us home.

Ezekiel 34:11–16
Psalm 23
Romans 5:5b–11
Luke 15:3–7

Saturday

JUNE 8

• THE IMMACULATE HEART OF THE BLESSED VIRGIN MARY •

"Thank God! Give him the praise and the glory. Before all the living,
acknowledge the many good things he has done for you, by blessing and
extolling his name in song."
—TOBIT 12:6–7

Immaculate: stainless, flawless, without sin, pure of heart,
perfect love for God, a love for Jesus that was holy and
immense, the way God most desires to be loved in total
devotion. Mary is an example for the way we, too, may love
God—immaculately.

Tobit 12:1, 5–15, 20
Tobit 13:2, 6–8
Luke 2:41–51

When the Lord saw her, he was moved with pity for her and said to her,
"Do not weep."
—LUKE 7:13

In both the Old Testament and New Testament readings
today, a widow has lost her son. And in both instances,
God looks on her with compassion and restores the son to
life. How this loss—the loss of a son—must resonate in
some mysterious way in the heavens. And, as with heaven's
story, sons are restored and resurrected. Heaven's story is
our story; one day, our restoration will come.

1 Kings 17:17–24
Psalm 30
Galatians 1:11–19
Luke 7:11–17

"Blessed are the meek, / for they will inherit the land."
—MATTHEW 5:3

Fr. Adrian van Kaam writes, "The willful man squeezes every experience in a tight little box tied up with unbreakable strings. His mind becomes a storehouse of these little airtight compartments. He does not allow any new situation to touch the content of his store. . . . The gentle person is more free. He can take himself and the world as they are . . . It becomes easier for [them] to pray, to meditate, to stay attuned to God's presence. Gentility stills and quiets the greediness and aggressiveness of the ego." Thus the meek inherit the earth.

2 Corinthians 1:1–7
Psalm 34
Matthew 5:1–12

JUNE 11

• ST. BARNABAS, APOSTLE •

Then, completing their fasting and prayer, they laid hands on them and sent them off.
—ACTS 13:3

Do you have a difficult task ahead? An important decision to make? Have you been entrusted with a sick child or parent? Are you yourself ill, or ill at ease? We are never alone in the life God has given us at this moment. Gather your holiest friends, fast and pray together, let them lay their hands on you and ask the Holy Spirit to heal you, protect you, and lead you on.

Acts 11:21b–26; 13:1–3
Psalm 98
Matthew 5:13–16

"I have come not to abolish but to fulfill."
—MATTHEW 5:17

To abolish or to fulfill? There is a measure of completion
implied in both, but one results in destruction and from the
other springs life, abundant life. Heaven is not the end of
time but the fullness of time. You and I were meant to dwell
in that perfection, the completion of all that is to be
fulfilled.

2 Corinthians 3:4–11
Psalm 99
Matthew 5:17–19

JUNE 13

• ST. ANTHONY OF PADUA, PRIEST AND DOCTOR OF THE CHURCH •

"Go first and be reconciled with your brother."
—MATTHEW 5:24

The line for daily confession in my local church is always long. Someone is always turned away before Mass, and you can almost see the visible slump of disappointment. It is beautiful and humbling to see someone who takes seriously his or her need to be properly prepared and spiritually ready to receive the Blessed Sacrament, not out of scrupulosity but out of reverence and love. The difference is palpable.

2 Corinthians 3:15—4:1, 3–6
Psalm 85
Matthew 5:20–26

Friday

JUNE 14

"If your right eye causes you to sin, tear it out and throw it away."
—MATTHEW 5:29

"All exaggerations are true," wrote G. K. Chesterton, "if they exaggerate the right things." When Jesus exaggerates, we need to pay attention. He never backs away from pointing out the deadly serious danger of sin, maybe because it's so easy for us to rationalize about it. His hyperbole is not accidental, and while he does not wish us to disfigure our bodies, it's equally true that the condition of our souls is more important than anything else.

2 Corinthians 4:7–15
Psalm 116
Matthew 5:27–32

JUNE 15

*Whoever is in Christ is a new creation: the old things have passed
away; behold, new things have come.*
—2 CORINTHIANS 5:17

A friend of mine was terribly abused by her mother, a
mentally ill alcoholic. Her childhood was a nightmare of
neglect and meanness. My friend grew up, became a
Christian, married a decent man, and went on to have four
daughters of her own. She reports that with every act of
kindness and care, every maternal gentleness she shows her
daughters, a little more of her is healed. Moment by
moment, the old passes away. Bit by bit, someone new
is born.

2 Corinthians 5:14–21
Psalm 103
Matthew 5:33–37

Sunday

JUNE 16

"Her many sins have been forgiven because she has shown great love."
—LUKE 7:46

The *Redemptoris Mater* chapel contains the scene in mosaic. A
woman, clothed in gray, her features hidden from us,
rendering her anonymous, uses her hair to dry Christ's feet
after washing them in her tears of repentance and gratitude.
    She is bent low before the Messiah, who receives her
affection completely. Her contrition, vulnerable and heroic,
is met with great tenderness. All earnest confession is.

2 Samuel 12:7–10, 13
Psalm 32
Galatians 2:16, 19–21
Luke 7:36—8:3 or 7:36–50

"Offer no resistance to one who is evil. When someone strikes you on your right cheek, turn the other one to him as well."
—MATTHEW 5:39

In one of the first sermons I ever heard preached by my brother, a priest, he explained the difficult sentiment of this passage: in that moment when we "turn our cheek," we are confessing our hope that maybe the one who strikes us will repent. We are leaning in the direction of that person's conversion. And there is tremendous power in such a witness, power enough to push back a hateful hand, power enough to convert the hardest heart.

2 Corinthians 6:1–10
Psalm 98
Matthew 5:38–42

JUNE 18

The LORD sets captives free.
—PSALM 146:7

A young man I know was engaged to a beautiful young woman. But he was very much troubled by the fact that she would never leave the house without primping for hours.

There were no chains on her, but she was enslaved nonetheless—perhaps by her own vanity or the opinion of others. Her obsession with her own looks became so torturous that it eventually ended their engagement. All sin pushes true love away.

Lord, free me from all that keeps me enslaved to sin.

2 Corinthians 8:1–9
Psalm 146
Matthew 5:43–48

God loves a cheerful giver.
—2 CORINTHIANS 9:7

A monk was headed to his holy hour when there was a knock at the monastery door. A homeless man had been injured and needed treatment. Since the monk had been an infantry medic during the war, his fellow monks brought the man to him. He thought, *I'll miss my precious hour with Jesus,* but he tended to the man nonetheless. As he did so, he had the most distinct impression that he had spent a holy hour with Jesus indeed.

2 Corinthians 9:6–11
Psalm 112
Matthew 6:1–6, 16–18

I will give thanks to the LORD with all my heart.
—PSALM 111:1

There was the time my friend came and held my feet when
I had to be in the MRI tube for two hours. Or the time a
family that barely knew me invited me to dinner because I
was new in town. Or the extraordinary gift of a number of
very small children who have prayed for me spontaneously,
at no prodding of their parents.

We say "thank you" in the way we live and in the way
we receive.

2 Corinthians 11:1–11
Psalm 111
Matthew 6:7–15

"For where your treasure is, there also will your heart be."
—MATTHEW 6:21

Augustine writes in *City of God*, "If we are to discover the character of any people, we have only to examine what it loves." These questions are as helpful as any in preparing for confession: what do I love and how do I love it? In *Confessions* Augustine borrows from the Song of Songs: *ordinate in me caritatem*, "set charity to right in me," or order my loves. It is the prayer of every sinner turned saint.

2 Corinthians 11:18, 21–30
Psalm 34
Matthew 6:19–23

That I might not become too elated, a thorn in the flesh was given to me . . . Three times I begged the Lord about this, that it might leave me, but he said to me, "My grace is sufficient for you, for power is made perfect in weakness."
—2 CORINTHIANS 12:7–9

Here we are offered one possible explanation for evil and suffering. Not every "thorn in the flesh" is given by God to strengthen us, but some are. Can you think of things you have suffered that you know made you stronger, better, wiser, more grateful, more compassionate? Can you thank God for whatever you might be suffering now for the ways it could be perfecting you in Christ?

2 Corinthians 12:1–10
Psalm 34
Matthew 6:24–34

Once when Jesus was praying in solitude . . .
—LUKE 9:18

Once while on retreat I met a businessman who began each morning by committing to God every meeting he had that day. He was a leading executive, and his day was filled with back-to-back events, multimillion-dollar decisions that would affect the lives of many. In prayer and solitude he would tick down the list of appointments, presenting each of the people involved to the heart of Jesus.

Zechariah 12:10–11; 13:1
Psalm 63
Galatians 3:26–29
Luke 9:18–24

JUNE 24

• THE NATIVITY OF ST. JOHN THE BAPTIST •

Truly you have formed my inmost being;
you knit me in my mother's womb . . .

My soul also you knew full well;
nor was my frame unknown to you
When I was made in secret,
when I was fashioned in the depths of the earth.
—PSALM 139:13–15

Should all the world misunderstand you, should all the world misjudge you, God knows you. He sees you perfectly.

Vigil:	**Day:**
Jeremiah 1:4–10	Isaiah 49:1–6
Psalm 71	Psalm 139
1 Peter 1:8–12	Acts 13:22–26
Luke 1:5–17	Luke 1:57–66, 80

JUNE 25

How narrow the gate and constricted the road that leads to life. And those who find it are few.
—MATTHEW 7:14

Jesus, am I one of the few? Can I squeeze through the narrow gate that leads to life? The gate is narrow not because God is not generous, but because the sacrifices required—my pride, ego, vanity, selfishness, and sin—burden me and widen the self. Where God is, there is no room for anything else. Everything that is not God must be jettisoned for this, our most important journey.

Genesis 13:2, 5–18
Psalm 15
Matthew 7:6, 12–14

By their fruits you will know them.
—MATTHEW 7:20

May I be known, O Lord, by good and holy fruits grown
under your care.

Genesis 15:1–12, 17–18
Psalm 105
Matthew 7:15–20

"Everyone who listens to these words of mine and acts on them will be like a wise man who built his house on rock. The rain fell, the floods came, and the winds blew and buffeted the house. But it did not collapse; it had been set solidly on rock."
—MATTHEW 7:24–25

The Catholic Church teaches that the Eucharist is the source and summit of our faith. The Church must always return to the source of inspiration, which is the unending love of God most perfectly expressed in eucharistic love. The Eucharist is love that pours itself out in pure gift. This is the foundation on which we build our lives.

Genesis 16:1–12, 15–16 or 16:6–12, 15–16
Psalm 106
Matthew 7:21–29

Friday

JUNE 28

• ST. IRENAEUS, BISHOP AND MARTYR •

And then a leper approached, did him homage, and said, "Lord, if you wish, you can make me clean." He stretched out his hand, touched him, and said, "I will do it. Be made clean." His leprosy was cleansed immediately.
—MATTHEW 8:2–3

May we approach you, healing Lord, with whatever is not clean or well or whole. May we recognize in you the one who can, with one touch, change everything.

Genesis 17:1, 9–10, 15–22
Psalm 128
Matthew 8:1–4

Saturday

JUNE 29

• ST. PETER AND ST. PAUL, APOSTLES •

I want you to know, brothers and sisters, that the Gospel preached by me is not of human origin. For I did not receive it from a human being, nor was I taught it, but it came through a revelation of Jesus Christ.
—GALATIANS 1:11–12

Today, spend some time contemplating the origin of Scripture. What does it mean to you that you form your life and day on the word of God?

Vigil:	**Day:**
Acts 3:1–10	Acts 12:1–11
Psalm 19	Psalm 34
Galatians 1:11–20	2 Timothy 4:6–8, 17–18
John 21:15–19	Matthew 16:13–19

JUNE 30

For you were called for freedom, brothers and sisters. But do not use this freedom as an opportunity for the flesh; rather, serve one another through love.
—GALATIANS 5:13

Throughout his pontificate, Pope John Paul II continually reminded us that we "cannot fully find [ourselves] except through a sincere gift of [self]." Freedom and service are inseparable in the life of the spirit. Freedom for the Christian also means responsibility, even obligation, and ultimately deep and abiding joy in holding to that responsibility. Our gifts are given to us to be given away, and isn't that so much more freeing and joyful?

1 Kings 19:16b, 19–21
Psalm 16
Galatians 5:1, 13–18
Luke 9:51–62

Abraham drew nearer to him and said, "Will you sweep away the innocent with the guilty? Suppose there were fifty innocent people in the city . . . What if only forty . . . What if there are at least ten there?" The [Lord] replied, "For the sake of those ten, I will not destroy it."
—GENESIS 18:20–32

Abraham is baffled at the Lord's mathematics. He goes on and on, shrinking the numbers of the innocent—fifty, forty, thirty—and still the Lord persists in saving them. God's ways are not ours—he does not treat the human person as a commodity to be traded or used. He does not apply us to flowcharts and economic graphs. He forgives and saves us.

You are not God's commodity; you are his beloved child. He would save only you.

Genesis 18:16–33
Psalm 103
Matthew 8:18–22

JULY 2

Search me, O LORD, and try me;
test my soul and my heart.
—PSALM 26:2

I won't stand the test, but still I rest in this searching Jesus.
The truth about ourselves is a great gift and will always
bring freedom. We ask God to search us because in his
mercy, he will reveal all we need to know in each moment,
to continue to grow more like him. Self-awareness and
self-understanding are important means by which God
allows us to grow more freely toward heaven. We must
become willing to see ourselves through the eyes of Jesus.

Genesis 19:15–29
Psalm 26
Matthew 8:23–27

Then he said to Thomas, "Put your finger here and see my hands, and bring your hand and put it into my side, and do not be unbelieving, but believe." Thomas answered and said to him, "My Lord and my God!" Jesus said to him, "Have you come to believe because you have seen me? Blessed are those who have not seen and have believed."
—JOHN 20:27–28

Poor Thomas, held up as an example of "what not to do" for millennia to come. It's only human to doubt and want evidence. Jesus must have loved Thomas greatly to chasten him so publicly. Jesus must have known how it would hurt—and how many of us are exactly like Thomas.

My Lord and my God, you know my faith is sometimes feeble. In your mercy, grant me a stronger, believing heart.

Ephesians 2:19–22
Psalm 117
John 20:24–29

JULY 4

Let the peace of Christ control your hearts.
—COLOSSIANS 3:15

God is not afraid. He is not anxious. He doesn't worry or fret. The only possible item on God's agenda is to love you. May that be our guiding principle every moment: that we are loved completely and always. May that grow into an abiding peace in our families, our workplace, our country. May the peace of Christ overcome every darkened and abandoned corner of the world.

Isaiah 32:15–18, 20
Psalm 72:1–2, 3–4, 7–8, 12–13, 17
Colossians 3:12–15
John 20:19–23

Friday

JULY 5

Then Isaac took Rebekah into his tent; he married her and thus she became his wife. In his love for her, Isaac found solace after the death of his mother Sarah.
—GENESIS 24:67

When we are grieving or low, when we are wounded and in need of tenderness, we may find solace, comfort, and peace in loving those God gives to us.

Genesis 23:1–4, 19; 24:1–8, 62–67
Psalm 106
Matthew 9:9–13

"The LORD, your God, let things turn out well with me."
—GENESIS 27: 20

Maria Goretti forgave her would-be rapist from her deathbed; because of her purity and mercy, the Church declared her a saint. Sometimes we are mightily confused about what is important. But Maria was not confused. She knew that her body did not belong to a violent man. Her body did not even belong to her—it belonged to God and was meant for his glory, and entrusted to him, all things would turn out for the greater good.

Genesis 27:1–5, 15–29
Psalm 135
Matthew 9:14–17

Sunday

JULY 7

*As a mother comforts her child,
so will I comfort you.*
—ISAIAH 66:13

It is no small thing that motherhood is tied up with the
centerpiece of salvation history. No small thing that
Scripture is replete with feminine images of divine beauty
and strength. Who are the women around you who might
need reminding that their gifts are welcome and deeply
needed in the world?

Isaiah 66:10–14
Psalm 66
Galatians 6:14–18
Luke 10:1–12, 17–20 or 10:1–9

JULY 8

A woman suffering hemorrhages for twelve years came up behind him and touched the tassel on his cloak. She said to herself, "If only I can touch his cloak, I shall be cured."
—MATTHEW 9:20–21

The woman touched Jesus'cloak and was healed. It is difficult for us to take in the full gravity of the woman's actions. For touching a man she did not know, she might have lost her hand. Jesus knew that she was risking a great deal. There was acknowledgment in his reply, but no reproach, only healing. God knows when we are reaching for him. He knows better than we do how much we need his healing touch.

Reach, and you shall be cured.

Genesis 28:10–22a
Psalm 91
Matthew 9:18–26

Tuesday
JULY 9

At the sight of the crowds, his heart was moved with pity for them because they were like sheep without a shepherd. Then he said to his disciples, "The harvest is abundant but the laborers are few; so ask the master of the harvest to send out laborers for his harvest."
—MATTHEW 9:37–38

Vocations are a mercy granted by the master of the harvest. Today let's give thanks for all who have served as shepherds to us and ask the master to send more worthy men and women into the field.

Genesis 32:23–33
Psalm 17
Matthew 9:32–38

JULY 10

The plan of the LORD stands forever,
the design of his heart, through all generations.
—PSALM 33:11

From sunrise to sunset, from east to west, throughout all
eternity, you are woven into the design of God's heart.

Genesis 41:55–57; 42:5–7a, 17–24a
Psalm 33
Matthew 10:1–7

Thursday

JULY 11

• ST. BENEDICT, ABBOT •

"But now do not be distressed, and do not reproach yourselves for having sold me here. It was really for the sake of saving lives that God sent me here ahead of you."
—GENESIS 45:5

These are the words Joseph offers to his brothers who had sold him into slavery. Joseph offers a profound witness to the spiritual axiom that God can redeem any situation and convert any heart. There is no circumstance beyond his grasp, nothing he cannot transform to our good and the good of others, no betrayal that cannot be forgiven in complete freedom and love if we choose to lean in heaven's direction.

Genesis 44:18–21, 23–29; 45:1–5
Psalm 105
Matthew 10:7–15

Be shrewd as serpents and simple as doves.
—MATTHEW 10:16

Blessed John Henry Newman would say, "I want an educated laity." Indeed, nowhere in Scripture are we given a pass from study and understanding. At no time does Jesus indicate that faith should be severed from reason or that reason should be exalted above faith. Rather, they are a perfect paradoxical pairing resulting in a dynamic tension that gives life and fluidity to the Church and addresses the complex needs of the human spirit.

Genesis 46:1–7, 28–30
Psalm 37
Matthew 10:16–23

"God will surely take care of you and lead you out of this land to the land that he promised."
—GENESIS 50:24

God will take care of you. He will lead you out of this land—sickness, grieving, financial stress, troubled relationships, addiction, infertility, loneliness, friendlessness, betrayal, boredom, rejection, feeling overwhelmed, invisible, confused, uncertain, or unlovable. God's word is true, and he will lead you to a land of promise and peace.

Genesis 49:29–32; 50:15–26a
Psalm 105
Matthew 10:24–33

JULY 14

*"It is not up in the sky . . . Nor is it across the sea . . . No, it is
something very near to you, already in your mouths and in your hearts;
you have only to carry it out."*
—DEUTERONOMY 30:11–14

John of the Cross writes, "God . . . is hidden in the soul,
and there the good contemplative must seek him with
love . . . you yourself are his dwelling and his secret inner
room and hiding place . . . Desire him there, adore him
there. Do not go in pursuit of him outside yourself." Indeed,
right now, where you sit, you have all you need to listen to
and to hear the voice of the Lord.

Deuteronomy 30:10–14
Psalm 69 or 19
Colossians 1:15–20
Luke 10:25–37

Pharaoh then commanded all his subjects, "Throw into the river every boy that is born to the Hebrews."
—EXODUS 1:22

This evil is ancient. Life is vulnerable in every age. Every era has found ways to destroy new life, to crush those who are innocent, vulnerable, weak, and poor.

Lord, give us courage to protect all that you have created. Give us the grace to walk firmly in the conviction that all life is precious, and help us do what it takes to protect those who cannot protect themselves.

Exodus 1:8–14, 22
Psalm 124
Matthew 10:34—11:1

Tuesday

JULY 16

• OUR LADY OF MOUNT CARMEL •

I am afflicted and in pain;
let your saving help, O God, protect me.
—PSALM 69:29

What is your affliction? What's the nature of your pain?
Such a great freedom in the Christian life is unveiled by the
lamenting psalmist; we may cry out to God in any
condition. There is no circumstance that is off-limits, no
topic taboo, no problem we are left to solve on our own.
Nothing need be hidden from God.

Exodus 2:1–15a
Psalm 69
Matthew 11:20–24

But Moses said to God, "Who am I that I should go to Pharaoh and lead the children of Israel out of Egypt?" [God] answered, "I will be with you."
—EXODUS 3:11

No doubt you've heard that "God never gives us more than we can handle." This is not my experience! God seems always to be giving us more than we can handle. It's just never more than *God* can handle. Moses understood. He knew he wasn't qualified, that he wasn't enough. God made him enough. God reminded him, "I will be with you." That's why we can handle more than we can handle, because God is right here with us.

Exodus 3:1–6, 9–12
Psalm 103
Matthew 11:25–27

"I am meek and humble of heart."
—MATTHEW 11:29

We confuse meekness with weakness, rushing off to
assertiveness training so that we can negotiate better
salaries and more important positions in the world. We
strive and grasp—and have no rest. Jesus grasps at nothing.
He is meek and humble of heart. That's why we rest in him.

Just for today, let it all go. Be meek. Let the world swirl
around you. Rest in the humble heart of Jesus.

Exodus 3:13–20
Psalm 105
Matthew 11:28–30

"I desire mercy, not sacrifice."
—MATTHEW 12:7

What's the difference between mercy and sacrifice? Heart.
Jesus is quoting Hosea, who was chastising the people for
carrying out religious rituals without any heart. Ritual is
meaningless unless we understand the heart-principle
behind it. Our dogmas and doctrines are deeply important,
but they are real and lasting only when they are informed
by love. Going through the motions takes us only so far. If
you catch yourself in this posture, stop, take a breath, and
ask the Holy Spirit to quicken your heart.

Exodus 11:10—12:14
Psalm 116
Matthew 12:1–8

Who split the Red Sea in twain,
for his mercy endures forever;
And led Israel through its midst,
for his mercy endures forever;
But swept Pharaoh and his army into the Red Sea,
for his mercy endures forever.
—PSALM 136:13–15

A cartoon: in the background, Pharaoh and his army are being swallowed up by the Red Sea; in the foreground, an Israelite coming up from the water, having been brought to miraculous safety and rescued from certain death, turns to his companion and says, "Oh ick, I stepped on a fish." Good thing, God's mercy endures forever.

Exodus 12:37–42
Psalm 136
Matthew 12:14–21

JULY 21

"*Martha, you are anxious and worried about many things. There is need of only one thing. Mary has chosen the better part and it will not be taken from her.*"
—LUKE 10:41–42

There's nothing wrong with Martha's desire to be hospitable; each of us must take up the daily chores of living. But we might think of it this way: when we awake in the morning, before taking on the tasks of the day, let's sit first at the feet of Jesus—in prayer, sacred reading, meditation, and thanksgiving. Our first priority must be to sit at the feet of Jesus and then proceed to action.

Genesis 18:1–10a
Psalm 15
Colossians 1:24–28
Luke 10:38–42

JULY 22

• ST. MARY MAGDALENE •

"I sought him, / whom my heart loves. . . . / I found him whom my heart loves."
—SONG OF SONGS 3:1–4

John of the Cross said it this way: "If anyone is seeking God, the Beloved is seeking that person much more. . . . He acts as guide of the blind, leading it by the hand to the place it knows not how to reach." There is something of Mary Magdalene's story in this: seeking and finding because she was first sought. Something of my story, too.

Song of Songs 3:1–4 or 1 Corinthians 5:14–17
Psalm 63
John 20:1–2, 11–18

"For whoever does the will of my heavenly Father is my brother, and sister, and mother."
—MATTHEW 12:50

It's not so much that old familial ties are abolished and new bonds are made as much as a new order visits the family of God. A great sweeping community is established by the heavenly Father. Jesus does not reject human bonds; he exalts heavenly ones.

Exodus 14:21—15:1
Exodus 15:8–9, 10, 12, 17
Matthew 12:46–50

Then the LORD said to Moses, "I will now rain down bread from
heaven for you."
—EXODUS 16:4

God's response to the grumbling Israelites: bread from
heaven. You have to wonder why he put up with them!
What do these grousing complainers have to teach me? In
what ways has God's mercy rained down on me? In what
desert places of my life has he rescued me with the most
unlikely provision?

Today, I will remember God's mercies even in the face of
my complaints, and give thanks.

Exodus 16:1–5, 9–15
Psalm 78
Matthew 13:1–9

Thursday

JULY 25

We are . . . always carrying about in the body the dying of Jesus, so that the life of Jesus may also be manifest in our body. For we who live are constantly being given up to death for the sake of Jesus so that the life of Jesus may be manifested in our mortal flesh.
—2 CORINTHIANS 4:8, 11

There is a religious order devoted to precisely this: the Passionists strive to keep the love of the crucified Jesus as seen in his sacred passion alive and real to the world. Their motto is "May the passion of Christ be always in our hearts." How can I make the saving passion of Jesus more real to the world? How can I carry him more and more in my life, in my person?

2 Corinthians 4:7–15
Psalm 126
Matthew 20:20–28

Friday

JULY 26

*Honor your father and your mother, that you may have a long life in
the land which the LORD, your God, is giving you.*
—EXODUS 20:12

It's a tough gig to be a good parent. To raise a child well, to
help prepare the child for his or her calling. Pope Benedict
XVI once said that if we teach our children to pray, we can
trust them with their vocation. Let's teach our children
to pray.

Exodus 20:1–17
Psalm 19
Matthew 13:18–23

God the LORD has spoken and summoned the earth,
from the rising of the sun to its setting.
From Zion, perfect in beauty,
God shines forth.
—PSALM 50:1–2

My favorite panel in the Sistine Chapel is the one of God creating night and day. It depicts a commanding, ancient figure, perfectly and without hesitation, appointing the sun and the moon to their places. Beautiful, powerful, glorious.

Exodus 24:3–8
Psalm 50
Matthew 13:24–30

"If you then, who are wicked, know how to give good gifts to your children, how much more will the Father in heaven give the Holy Spirit to those who ask him?"
—LUKE 11:13

I might ask for a house, a husband, my health, or the flourishing of my friends. I might ask for greater faith or an end to abortion and capital punishment. I might ask for help and forgiveness for some sin or the capacity to forgive a painful offense. Our prayer is not about getting what we want—though sometimes we do get precisely what we ask for. Prayer is about receiving the One who is sent to attend our prayers.

Genesis 18:20–32
Psalm 138
Colossians 2:12–14
Luke 11:1–13

Jesus told her, "I am the resurrection and the life; whoever believes in me, even if he dies, will live, and anyone who lives and believes in me will never die. Do you believe this?" [Martha] said to him, "Yes, Lord. I have come to believe that you are the Christ."
—JOHN 11:25–26

For some people, conversion is instantaneous and lasting, but for most of us belief develops gradually. Martha's witness is an excellent example of this fact. The life of faith is a constant movement toward deeper and deeper faith. Martha needed to learn moment by moment how to choose "the better part" that Mary did when she sat at the feet of Jesus. Martha came to believe day by day in spending more time with Jesus, and so will we.

Exodus 32:15–24, 30–34
Psalm 106
John 11:19–27 or Luke 10:38–42

The LORD used to speak to Moses face to face, as one man speaks to another.
—EXODUS 33:11

Extraordinary. Imagine such an encounter!

The Lord speaks to me face-to-face too—in adoration, in the eyes of the poor, in the beauties of the earth, in prayer and quiet places.

Lord, where are you speaking to me face-to-face?

Exodus 33:7–11; 34:5b–9, 28
Psalm 103
Matthew 13:36–43

Wednesday

JULY 31

"When he finds a pearl of great price, he goes and sells all that he has and buys it."
—MATTHEW 13:46

St. Ignatius reminds us, "Few men suspect what God would make them if they placed no obstacle to His work." What keeps me from my pearl of great price, from following Jesus with everything that I am, everything I have, every thought and movement of my mind and heart? Lord, let me lean more into your generosity, trusting, as Ignatius put it: "The more the soul attaches itself to God and shows itself generous toward Him, the more apt it becomes to receive graces and spiritual gifts in abundance."

Exodus 34:29–35
Psalm 99
Matthew 13:44–46

AUGUST 1

• ST. ALPHONSUS LIGUORI, BISHOP AND DOCTOR OF THE CHURCH •

My soul yearns and pines / for the courts of the LORD.
—PSALM 84:3

Loveliness is essential in the Christian life; rightly received, it draws us nearer to the transcendent. Gesa Elsbeth Thiessen says it this way: "The magnitude of beauty in nature and in all human creation, wherever it is experienced, gives us a glimpse of the beauty of God, therein lies its saving power." Thomas Aquinas noted that the beautiful should never be an "innocuous sedative," but an evocation of the "good made visible."

Lord, may my life be beautiful, your goodness made visible.

Exodus 40:16–21, 34–38
Psalm 84
Matthew 13:47–53

He did not work many mighty deeds there because of their lack of faith.
—MATTHEW 13:58

How much faith do I need for God to act? Do I need mighty faith for mighty deeds? Will Jesus come, even when I barely muster a feeble prayer?

The lack of faith expressed in this passage was accompanied by open antagonism. These people "took offense" when Jesus preached and healed. The Lord will meet me in my faith though it is like a mustard seed, but he will never force himself upon my heart.

Leviticus 23:1, 4–11, 15–16, 27, 34–37
Psalm 81
Matthew 13:54–58

"This fiftieth year you shall make sacred by proclaiming liberty in the land for all its inhabitants. It shall be a jubilee for you, when every one of you shall return to his own property, every one to his own family estate."
—LEVITICUS 25:10

According to the laws of the day, land wasn't exactly purchased and sold as a permanent transaction; it was much more akin to leasing. Land retained its ties to a family, even if they were not currently living on it, hence the return to the "family estate" during the jubilee year. This practice emphasized for the Israelites the fact that no one really owned the land; rather, everything belonged to God. Indeed, all our blessings belong first to God.

Leviticus 25:1, 8–17
Psalm 67
Matthew 14:1–12

"But God said to him, 'You fool, this night your life will be demanded of you; and the things you have prepared, to whom will they belong?' Thus will it be for all who store up treasure for themselves but are not rich in what matters to God."
—LUKE 12:20–21

Carlo Carretto writes that "Riches are a slow poison, which strikes almost imperceptibly, paralyzing the soul at the moment when it seems healthiest." Do I make a practice of relaxing my grip on those things that plant my energies firmly in this world and not in the next? How much time do I devote each day to matters important to God? Do those same things matter to me?

Ecclesiastes 1:2; 2:21–23
Psalm 90
Colossians 3:1–5, 9–11
Luke 12:13–21

• THE DEDICATION OF THE BASILICA OF ST. MARY MAJOR •

My people heard not my voice,
and Israel obeyed me not;
So I gave them up to the hardness of their hearts;
they walked according to their own counsels.
—PSALM 81:12–13

When I get willful, I become colossally stupid. Turning my nose up at heaven and going my own way not only cuts me off from God's wisdom and grace, but also it very often lands me in dim-witted messes that damage me and the people around me.

Lord, protect me from the hardened stupidity of my willfulness that turns away your wisdom. Let my first and last counsel always be your counsel.

Numbers 11:4b–15
Psalm 81
Matthew 14:13–21

His dominion is an everlasting dominion / that shall not be taken away,
/ his kingship shall not be destroyed.
—DANIEL 7:14

Which is another way of saying, "This is my chosen Son;
listen to him."

Daniel 7:9–10, 13–14
Psalm 97
2 Peter 1:16–19
Luke 9:28b–36

⇒ 248 ⇐

Then Jesus said to her in reply, "O woman, great is your faith!"
—MATTHEW 15:28

Take note of how countercultural Jesus was with women; he taught them, allowed them to accompany him, first appeared to women after his resurrection, healed them and loved them, and praised them for their faith. Far from being indifferent or oppressive, Jesus extends women enormous dignity and worth.

Pick a woman who has been instrumental in your faith life. In a way of your choosing, bestow upon her this same dignity and acknowledgment.

Numbers 13:1–2, 25—14:1 26–29, 34–35
Psalm 106
Matthew 15:21–28

AUGUST 8

• ST. DOMINIC, PRIEST •

*"Get behind me, Satan! You are an obstacle to me. You are thinking not
as God does, but as human beings do."*
—MATTHEW 16:23

Once when I was facing grave illness, a well-meaning friend
said, "Well, life's a tragedy and your life is marked by it
more than most." I thought, *Get behind me, stupid man! My life is
not a tragedy, but a triumph—even this illness—in Christ.* My
sufferings do nothing but make me richer and more real;
they provide an extraordinary opportunity to know Jesus in
one of the most intimate ways he may be known: in
suffering.

Numbers 20:1–13
Psalm 95
Matthew 16:13–23

Jesus said to his disciples, "Whoever wishes to come after me must deny himself, take up his cross, and follow me. For whoever wishes to save his life will lose it, but whoever loses his life for my sake will find it."
—MATTHEW 16:24–25

Before Edith Stein lost her life in a concentration camp, this philosopher-Carmelite wrote, "The deepest longing of a woman's heart is to give herself lovingly, to belong to another, and to possess this other being completely. This longing is revealed in her outlook, personal, and all-embracing . . . Only God can welcome a person's total surrender in such a way that one does not lose one's soul in the process but wins it."

Deuteronomy 4:32–40
Psalm 77
Matthew 16:24–28

"Amen, amen, I say to you, unless a grain of wheat falls to the ground and dies, it remains just a grain of wheat; but if it dies, it produces much fruit."
—JOHN 12:24

Death to sin; death to self; death to my own presumption, pride, and judgments on the heart of another. Death to fear; death to boredom; death to despair and discontent; death to joylessness, apathy, and anxiety.

Death to all that keeps me from an abundant life with you, Jesus.

2 Corinthians 9:6–10
Psalm 112
John 12:24–26

Sunday

AUGUST 11

*Much will be required of the person entrusted with much, and still more
will be demanded of the person entrusted with more.*
—LUKE 12:48

What is my "more"? Health, wealth, education, raw
intelligence? A particular sensitivity to the suffering of
others? The ability to listen well, teach the truth, or remain
faithful? A poverty of spirit, a deep prayer life, gratitude
even in the face of affliction? Am I offering to God all of
"the more" with which I've been entrusted?

Wisdom 18:6–9
Psalm 33
Hebrews 11:1–2, 8–19 or 11:1–2, 8–12
Luke 12:32–48 or 12:35–40

———————————

AUGUST 12

• ST. JANE FRANCES DE CHANTAL, RELIGIOUS •

You too must befriend the alien, for you were once aliens yourselves.
—DEUTERONOMY 10:19

Who among us does not know what it feels like to be a stranger in a strange land? Just as the Lord befriends us when no one else will, so we must turn to those around us who live on the fringe of society and invite them to our table.

If a stranger comes to my parish, will he or she feel welcome? Do I make a point to be hospitable to newcomers, visitors, strangers, or the marginalized in my circle of influence?

Deuteronomy 10:12–22
Psalm 147
Matthew 17:22–27

AUGUST 13

*Moses summoned Joshua and in the presence of all Israel said to him,
"Be brave and steadfast, for you must bring this people into the land . . .
of their heritage. It is the LORD who marches before you; he will be with
you and will never fail you or forsake you. So do not fear or
be dismayed."*
—DEUTERONOMY 31:7–8

Moses's work was done, and he handed the care of his people over to Joshua. Each of us must eventually pass on aspects of our work to another. Let us be especially mindful to do so with the same kind of encouragement and clarity Moses expressed: the Lord will never fail you or forsake you. Do not fear; he marches before you.

Deuteronomy 31:1–8
Deuteronomy 32:3–4, 7–9, 12
Matthew 18:1–5, 10, 12–14

AUGUST 14

• ST. MAXIMILIAN MARY KOLBE, PRIEST AND MARTYR •

"For where two or three are gathered together in my name, there am I in the midst of them."
—MATTHEW 18:20

Is Jesus suggesting that praying alone has less value or power? I think of my first prayer partner and one of my best friends, Pamela. Our prayer time together has bonded us in a way I experience with few others. Perhaps in one sense this passage emphasizes our human need for community, for communal participation in the Body of Christ. Together we can accomplish what we might never accomplish on our own.

Deuteronomy 34:1–12
Psalm 66:1–3, 5, 8, 16–17
Matthew 18:15–20

While Jesus was speaking, a woman from the crowd called out and said to him, "Blessed is the womb that carried you and the breasts at which you nursed." He replied, "Rather, blessed are those who hear the word of God and observe it."
—LUKE 11:27–28

In no way was Jesus diminishing the gift of Mary's motherhood; he was emphasizing the greater gift of her obedience and faithfulness. While Mary's place will always be unique in human history and in heaven, Jesus reminds us that each of us is given the opportunity to hear and obey the word of God. Mary, Mother of God, Queen of Heaven and Earth, pray for us.

Vigil:	**Day:**
1 Chronicles 15:3–4, 15, 16; 16:1–2	Revelation 11:19a; 12:1–6a, 10ab
Psalm 132	Psalm 45
1 Corinthians 15:54b–57	1 Corinthians 15:20–27
Luke 11:27–28	Luke 1:39–56

*Some . . . have renounced marriage for the sake of the Kingdom
of heaven.*
—MATTHEW 19:12

Every vocation calls for a renunciation. The married
renounce all others and their singular ambitions to build a
unity of two; a priest renounces being father to a few so
that he might be father to many; the consecrated renounce
marriage so that they may serve the Church with an
undivided heart, and so on. Today, spend some time
reflecting on whatever you may have renounced for the
sake of the kingdom of heaven.

Joshua 24:1–13
Psalm 136
Matthew 19:3–12

AUGUST 17

*"Decide today whom you will serve . . . As for me and my household, we
will serve the LORD."*
—JOSHUA 24:15

In philosophical terms, we know that love is an act of the
will. It is not simply a feeling or an emotion; it is a decision
you make in the deepest part of who you are. While
feelings and emotions are powerful and while they serve a
beautiful purpose, it is a relief to know that I do not have to
be dictated by them. And eventually, feeling follows act. If I
act lovingly, even when I don't feel like it, love will follow.

Joshua 24:14–29
Psalm 16
Matthew 19:13–15

AUGUST 18

"Do you think that I have come to establish peace on the earth? No, I tell you, but rather division. From now on a . . . father will be divided against his son and a son against his father, a mother against her daughter and a daughter against her mother."
—LUKE 12:51–53

We pray for unity within the human family, but not everyone will accept the Gospel message of repentance and mercy. We strive for peace and justice, knowing that these things may not come without great pain, division, loss, and strife, even under our own roofs. Lord, give us wisdom to know when to act as blessed peacemakers and when to embrace division for the kingdom's sake.

Jeremiah 38:4–6, 8–10
Psalm 40
Hebrews 12:1–4
Luke 12:49–53

AUGUST 19

• ST. JOHN EUDES, PRIEST •

"If you wish to be perfect, go, sell what you have and give to the poor, and you will have treasure in heaven. Then, come, follow me." When the young man heard this statement, he went away sad, for he had many possessions.
—MATTHEW 19:21–22

Lord, would I, too, go away sad? What are the "possessions" in my life that keep me from following you? Pride, money, vanity, a sense of security, fear? Lord, help me to let go of all that keeps me from going where you go.

Judges 2:11–19
Psalm 106
Matthew 19:16–22

AUGUST 20

• ST. BERNARD, ABBOT AND DOCTOR OF THE CHURCH •

And everyone who has given up houses or brothers or sisters or father or mother or children or lands for the sake of my name will receive a hundred times more.
—MATTHEW 19:29

When my brother entered seminary, I had a distinct sense of losing him. When he stepped from the altar after completing his first Mass, a friend noted that it was almost like he was saying good-bye. And it was beautiful. But there was more. I did lose a brother, but I gained many more: so many of his seminary brothers became my brothers, men I love and respect and relish just as much as my own flesh and blood. God is generous.

Judges 6:11–24a
Psalm 85
Matthew 19:23–30

AUGUST 21

• ST. PIUS X, POPE •

"Are you envious because I am generous?"
—MATTHEW 20:15

I was upset because with a certain friend, I had to do all the initiating, assume all the personal risk. I had to do more work than he did to keep us connected. My good girlfriend, married a long while and happily so, is good to remind me that relationships are not about parity; they are about self-gift. A generous heart is not interested in perfect equality but in perfect love.

Judges 9:6–15
Psalm 21
Matthew 20:1–16

AUGUST 22

• QUEENSHIP OF THE BLESSED VIRGIN MARY •

Many are invited, but few are chosen.
—MATTHEW 22:14

This hardly seems fair. Why invite someone only to
reject them?

The parables of Jesus are always trying to teach us
something about the ways of heaven. Here, the story tells
us that God's justice demands something of us, that we
accept Jesus without equivocation. Those who go
"unchosen" want to make adjustments to the plan of
salvation.

Judges 11:29–39
Psalm 40
Matthew 22:1–14

*"Wherever you go, I will go, wherever you lodge I will lodge, your
people shall be my people, and your God my God."*
—RUTH 1:16

Every time we witness an act of tremendous heroism in the
Bible, God is revealing some aspect of himself, some shade
of his love for us. This is Ruth's moment of conversion. She
was a woman without children—a great dishonor—a
widow, a foreigner. To stay with her mother-in-law, Naomi,
would likely mean tremendous hardship for her, but she was
determined not to abandon her mother-in-law. Ruth's
heroism is fed by heaven and reflects the love of God.

Ruth 1:1, 3–6, 14b–16, 22
Psalm 146
Matthew 22:34–40

Can anything good come from Nazareth?
—JOHN 1:46

This verse always cuts to the core of my presumption, my judgments and preconceived notions. When I think I know everything, when I think I have summed up some bit of suffering or difficulty as being entirely negative, hopeless, or useless, when I have passed judgment on another as useless, beneath me, inferior, of no consequence—in those moments, I beg God Almighty for the grace to be reminded, firmly if necessary, that my salvation rests in the Nazorean.

Revelation 21:9b–14
Psalm 145
John 1:45–51

AUGUST 25

Some of these I will take as priests.
—ISAIAH 66:21

He is still taking some as priests. As sisters, brothers, and monks. Today we pray for vocations to religious and consecrated life, all those who serve us with a singleness of purpose.

Isaiah 66:18–21
Psalm 117
Hebrews 12:5–7, 11–13
Luke 13:22–30

AUGUST 26

We give thanks to God always for all of you, remembering you in our prayers.
—1 THESSALONIANS 1:2

Where would I be without the prayers of my mother and father on my behalf? Their intercession is powerful and steadfast. Thank you, Mom and Dad.

Who prays for you? Whose intercession helps you stay upright? Remember them to God in gratitude.

1 Thessalonians 1:2–5, 8b–10
Psalm 149
Matthew 23:13–22

With such affection for you, we were determined to share with you not only the Gospel of God, but our very selves as well, so dearly beloved had you become to us.
—1 THESSALONIANS 2:8

Love will automatically build to a perfect sharing of self. Jesus gives himself to us in perfect friendship in all the sacraments, but especially in the Eucharist. How do I give myself? Where do I fan the flame of affection so that I can become a dearly beloved gift?

1 Thessalonians 2:1–8
Psalm 139
Matthew 23:23–26

If I take the wings of the dawn,
if I settle at the farthest limits of the sea,
Even there your hand shall guide me,
and your right hand hold me fast.
—PSALM 139:9–10

A woman was stricken with sudden blindness. Eventually her sight returned, and she gave thanks to God. Later, she was asked about this and why God did not heal her immediately when she asked. She said, "He did not take away my blindness, but rather, he came into the darkness with me."

1 Thessalonians 2:9–13
Psalm 139
Matthew 23:27–32

Thursday

AUGUST 29

To strengthen your hearts, to be blameless in holiness before our God and Father.
—1 THESSALONIANS 3:13

This is the mark of martyrs like St. John. to be strong in heart, blameless, and holy.

God, give me holy courage.

1 Thessalonians 3:7–13
Psalm 90
Mark 6:17–29

This is the will of God, your holiness.
—1 THESSALONIANS 4:3

What is holiness in 2013? Does it look any different today
than it did for the early church? Blessed John Paul II says,
"Holiness is to raise one's eyes to the summit. Holiness is
intimacy with God the Father who is in Heaven. In this
intimacy, each one of us is aware of our nature, with all its
limitations and difficulties." This is the will of God for us:
an intimate relationship with him in which we find grace
for our sanctification.

1 Thessalonians 4:1–8
Psalm 97
Matthew 25:1–13

*Since you were faithful in small matters, I will give you great
responsibilities. Come, share your master's joy.*
—MATTHEW 25:23

The parable of the talents always struck me as just a bit
harsh. The third servant played it safe and was punished for
it. Love is risky business. God doesn't want us to live in
chaos and imprudence, but neither does he want us to play
it safe. A faithful Christian life must involve some risk. A
girlfriend of mine says, "Write God a blank check," and
then just see what he does. Maybe sometimes, God writes
us a blank check, too.

1 Thessalonians 4:9–11
Psalm 98
Matthew 25:14–30

SEPTEMBER 1

My child conduct your affairs with humility,
and you will be loved more than a giver of gifts.
Humble yourself the more, the greater you are,
and you will find favor with God.
—SIRACH 3:17–18

Humility necessarily involves a certain kind of
self-forgetfulness in communion with an active
remembrance of God and his grace active in us.

Sirach 3:17–18, 20, 28–29
Psalm 68
Hebrews 12:18–19, 22–24
Luke 14:1, 7–14

For the Lord himself, with a word of command, with the voice of an archangel and with the trumpet of God, will come down from heaven, and the dead in Christ will rise first. Then we who are alive, who are left, will be caught up together with them in the clouds to meet the Lord in the air.

—1 THESSALONIANS 4:15–17

This passage speaks of the Second Coming. How much time do we spend thinking about the final things: heaven, hell, purgatory, the final judgment? It is good in this season, as fall arrives, to spend some time reflecting on the meaning of final things and how much of our lives are ordered toward heaven.

1 Thessalonians 4:13–18
Psalm 96
Luke 4:16–30

SEPTEMBER 3

• ST. GREGORY THE GREAT, POPE AND DOCTOR OF THE CHURCH •

Encourage one another and build one another up.
—1 THESSALONIANS 5:11

The word of God is a deep mystery, and at times it is very difficult to comprehend. At other times it's about as simple, gentle, and direct as can be. St. Gregory said it this way: "Those who love their friends in God and their enemies for God's sake possess true love."

Do I build up my brethren or spend my energies criticizing them? Do I encourage those around me in the faith? Do I remind people by the way I live and love that they are deeply loved by Jesus?

1 Thessalonians 5:1–6, 9–11
Psalm 27
Luke 4:31–37

Grace to you and peace from God our Father.
—COLOSSIANS 1:1

I love a good letter. The epistles are especially appealing because of their holy salutations. Note how often believers bless one another, pray for one another, and wish one another God's grace and every goodness. God's grace and blessing are infinitely abundant. How often do we call on them throughout our day on behalf of one another? Today, let's make a greater effort to call on the blessing of God Almighty for all people we encounter

Colossians 1:1–8
Psalm 52
Luke 4:38–44

SEPTEMBER 5

Jesus said to Simon, "Do not be afraid; from now on you will be catching men."
—LUKE 5:11

At my brother's ordination reception, the organizers had filled mason jars with water, put a fish in each one, and attached a note saying *Be fishers of men.* The gifts were meant for the children to take home, to stir their imaginations and spirits toward the possibility of vocations, but what a good reminder for all. We are not after health, wealth, or success, though these things can be great helps to us. We are all fishers of people. In our private, unique ways, let's go fishing today.

Colossians 1:9–14
Psalm 98
Luke 5:1–11

He is before all things,
and in him all things hold together.
—COLOSSIANS 1:17

God knows—before the plane goes down, the disease hits,
the economy tumbles, or your child grows ill. God's gaze
rests on you before the betrayal or the sin, before love dies
or grows stale, before your loneliness or selfishness, before
whatever season of suffering or strife may befall you. See
God's hands, strong and eternal and able, holding you up,
holding together you and yours— and the very world
around you.

Colossians 1:15–20
Psalm 100
Luke 5:33–39

SEPTEMBER 7

God has now reconciled you in the fleshly Body of Christ through his death, to present you holy, without blemish, and irreproachable before him, provided that you persevere in the faith, firmly grounded, stable, and not shifting from the hope of the Gospel.
—COLOSSIANS 1:22–23

Fixum est cor meum. My heart is steadfast, O Lord, my heart is set.

Jesus, my heart can be fickle and shifting. Help me to grow more steady. Keep me firmly grounded in you, my heart set upon you.

Colossians 1:21–23
Psalm 54
Luke 6:1–5

SEPTEMBER 8

Whoever does not carry his own cross and come after me cannot be my disciple. Which of you wishing to construct a tower does not first sit down and calculate the cost to see if there is enough for its completion?
—LUKE 14:28

Jesus desires for us to love through to completion, because that is the way he loves: completely, fully, to the end, to eternity.

Wisdom 9:13–18b
Psalm 90
Philemon 9–10, 12–17
Luke 14:25–33

Only in God be at rest, my soul,
for from him comes my hope.
—PSALM 62:5

Human optimism and divine hope are quite different; the
first looks to the earth and humanity and says, "We will
work hard to make things better." The second looks to
heaven and God and says, "In Christ, all things are
possible." Where is the source of the power to change? Is it
rooted in human optimism or divine hope? The great
mystery and delight of the Christian life is that we
cocreate. Jesus invites us to cooperate with his grace, and
this fills the heart with hope.

Colossians 1:24—2:3
Psalm 62
Luke 6:6–11

SEPTEMBER 10

Jesus departed to the mountain to pray, and he spent the night in prayer to God. When day came, he called his disciples to himself and from them he chose Twelve.
—LUKE 6:12

Prayer precedes every great work of Jesus. And it precedes the great works of the Church as well. As I watched my brother prepare for the priesthood, six years and then some, I became aware that it was not just my brother who was deciding to become a priest, but a body of men, the Church, those charged with his preparation, who agreed that he was called. They prayed and prepared, and when the day came, they called.

Colossians 2:6–15
Psalm 145
Luke 6:12–19

283

His greatness is unsearchable.
—PSALM 145:3

Lord, we look for you everywhere: in the miracles and
mysteries of life, death, and suffering; in the eyes of the
poor and those impoverished in spirit; in the kindness of
strangers and the courage of the heroic; in daybreak and in
sunset; in the beauties of heaven and earth; in the darkness
of human sin and human frailty and human hearts. We seek
you. We search for you and find you, but never fully and
never enough. And so we seek you still.

Colossians 3:1–11
Psalm 145
Luke 6:20–26

SEPTEMBER 12

• THE MOST HOLY NAME OF MARY •

Put on, as God's chosen ones, holy and beloved, heartfelt compassion,
kindness, humility, gentleness, and patience, bearing with one another
and forgiving one another . . . And over all these put on love, that is, the
bond of perfection.
—COLOSSIANS 2:12–14

Oh, profane and unloved, put on indifference, meanness, arrogance, harshness, impatience, unforgiveness, and hate.

Which list makes your heart lighten and sing? Carry it around in your heart's pocket today. Breathe it in. Let this little litany seep into the beating rhythm of life that moves you forward.

Colossians 3:12–17
Psalm 150
Luke 6:27–38

⇒ 285 ⇐

No disciple is superior to the teacher; but when fully trained, every disciple will be like his teacher.
—LUKE 6:40

St. John Chrysostom, often referred to as "golden-mouthed" for his stirring homilies, wrote, "It is not possible, I say *not possible*, ever to exhaust the mind of the Scriptures. It is a well which has no bottom."

We come to the Scriptures to spend more time with the Teacher. We come to enter our training. The sacraments and a holy life: these are our lessons.

1 Timothy 1:1–2, 12–14
Psalm 16
Luke 6:39–42

SEPTEMBER 14

• THE EXALTATION OF THE HOLY CROSS •

For God did not send his Son into the world to condemn the world, but that the world might be saved through him.
—JOHN 3:17

This is the work of the cross: to save you.

This is the work of the crucifixions of your life: to allow you to join in the saving work of the cross.

Spend some time in meditation before a crucifix today. Ask Jesus to show you what it means to you that he is there.

Numbers 21:4b–9
Psalm 78
Philippians 2:6–11
John 3:13–17

SEPTEMBER 15

*A clean heart create for me, O God,
and a steadfast spirit renew within me.*
—PSALM 51:10

Sin soils the soul. None of us escapes this. That's why
confession is so important and necessary. A priest I knew
who had received the stigmata said that after he received it,
he needed to go to confession far more often; he had a far
greater sensitivity to sin after receiving such an
extraordinary gift.

Make a commitment to receive the sacrament of
reconciliation at least once a month or more for the
next year.

Exodus 32:7–11, 13–14
Psalm 51
1 Timothy 1:12–17
Luke 15:1–32

• ST. CORNELIUS, POPE AND MARTYR • ST. CYPRIAN, BISHOP AND MARTYR •

"Lord, do not trouble yourself, for I am not worthy to have you enter under my roof. . . . but say the word and let my servant be healed. For I too am a person subject to authority, with soldiers subject to me. And I say to one, 'Go', and he goes; and to another, 'Come here' and he comes."
—LUKE 7:6–8

This passage goes on to describe Jesus' amazement at the faith of the centurion who has asked Jesus to heal his sick slave. Can you imagine amazing the King of Kings? How curious that a soldier who spends his day upholding military authority should so respect Christ's authority. Jesus is here to uphold the authority of his Father.

1 Timothy 2:1–8
Psalm 28
Luke 7:1–10

SEPTEMBER 17

• ST. ROBERT BELLARMINE, BISHOP AND DOCTOR OF THE CHURCH •

I will not set before my eyes
any base thing.
—PSALM 101:3

Matthew 6:22 says that the eye is the lamp of the body. We sometimes say it this way: the eyes are the window to the soul.

What are my windows letting in?

1 Timothy 3:1–13
Psalm 101
Luke 7:11–17

SEPTEMBER 18

Wisdom is vindicated by all her children.
—LUKE 7:35

I have too many children fathered by Folly and reared by
Selfishness. There would be more were it not for God's
mercy. I pray that more of my children are raised up by
Wisdom and Faith, Mercy and Hope.

1 Timothy 3:14–16
Psalm 111
Luke 7:31–35

"Two people were in debt to a certain creditor; one owed five hundred days' wages and the other owed fifty. Since they were unable to repay the debt, he forgave it for both. Which of them will love him more?"
—LUKE 7:41–42

The point is not who has sinned more or less. We all owe five hundred days' wages—and more; we all need much forgiveness. The point is how *we* can love more. We all owe a countless debt—one God will forgive in an instant. Therefore, we also have the capacity to show great love for God and for the people around us. Today, with full consciousness and intent, do not show a little love—show great love.

1 Timothy 4:12–16
Psalm 111
Luke 7:36–50

_____

• ST. ANDREW KIM TAE-GON, PRIEST AND MARTYR, ST. PAUL CHONG HA SANG, MARTYR, AND THEIR COMPANIONS, MARTYRS •

Mutual friction among people with corrupted mind, who are deprived of the truth.
—1 TIMOTHY 6:5

Here are the results when we reject the teaching of Christ: corruption, friction, and deprivation. They are ugly words, and I recoil from them. But how do we guard our minds against corruption? How do we protect ourselves from deprivation of the truth? Prayer, the Mass, the sacraments, holy friendships, Scripture study, sacred reading, adoration, and more prayer. Silence and meditation and the time we spend together each day.

1 Timothy 6:2c–12
Psalm 49
Luke 8:1–3

Grace was given to each of us according to the measure of Christ's gift.
And he gave some as Apostles, others as prophets, others as evangelists,
others as pastors and teachers, to equip the holy ones for the work of
ministry, for building up the Body of Christ.
—EPHESIANS 4:7, 11–12

Still others are gifted as artists and writers, others as
healers, others as intercessors and administrators, others as
musicians and liturgical ministers, all as witnesses, our gifts
given in service of the Body of Christ.

Ephesians 4:1–7, 11–13
Psalm 19
Matthew 9:9–13

SEPTEMBER 22

I ask that supplications, prayers, petitions, and thanksgivings be offered for everyone, for kings and for all in authority, that we may lead a quiet and tranquil life in all devotion and dignity.
—1 TIMOTHY 2:1

True leadership is a charism we can understand poorly. Jesus introduces us to servant-leadership by washing the feet of his disciples and dying on the cross. He was a living, radical reversal of all we understood of authority and the sacrifices inherent in it. Today, let us remember our Church and civic leaders in prayer, asking God to increase their strength, wisdom, courage, and loving stamina to lead as Christ leads and to serve as Christ serves.

Amos 8:4–7
Psalm 113
1 Timothy 2:1–8
Luke 16:1–13 or 16:10–13

*For there is nothing hidden that will not become visible, and nothing
secret that will not be known and come to light.*
—LUKE 8:17

St. Pio was well-known for his intolerance of poor
confessions. He would send away those whose confessions
were insincere, and recommended more frequent
confession: "Even a clean and unoccupied room gathers
dust; return after a week and you will see that it needs
dusting again!" We needn't fear Jesus' judgment; it will
always be a perfect coupling of justice and mercy. But we
are foolish to disregard the consequences of poor
confession—or no confession at all.

Ezra 1:1–6
Psalm 126
Luke 8:16–18

SEPTEMBER 24

My mother and my brothers are those who hear the word of God and act on it.
—LUKE 8:21

Here, when Jesus is told that his mother and brothers are outside, he does not reject his family but uses the moment to teach something about what matters most: the word and will of the Father. In a culture that values family ties to the exclusion of almost everything else, his statement is all the more emphatic.

Ezra 6:7–8, 12b, 14–20
Psalm 122
Luke 8:19–21

SEPTEMBER 25

Jesus summoned the Twelve and gave them power and authority.
—LUKE 9:1

Priests are not the only ones to whom God gives power and authority. And though we do not serve the Church in the same way priests do (with good reason), all the lay faithful are called to serve as priest, prophet, and king. The chief component of our priestly role is sacrificial. It is in the daily sacrifices we make, the ways in which we live our own lives a gift that Jesus gives us power and authority.

Ezra 9:5–9
Tobit 13:2, 3–4, 6–8
Luke 9:1–6

SEPTEMBER 26

• ST. COSMAS AND ST. DAMIAN, MARTYRS •

Now thus says the LORD of hosts: / Consider your ways! / You have sown much, but have brought in little; / you have eaten, but have not been satisfied; / You have drunk but have not been exhilarated; / have clothed yourselves, but not been warmed; / and whoever earned wages / earned them for a bag with holes in it.

—HAGGAI 1:5–6

Haggai is chastising the Israelites for allowing their discouragement to blossom into full-blown procrastination and avoidance. He is reminding all of us that our efforts at building a life without God will ultimately disappoint and dissatisfy. A holy life involves work. If we dedicate our works to God, they will ultimately build something lasting and eternal: virtue and holiness and love.

Haggai 1:1–8
Psalm 149
Luke 9:7–9

*Take courage, all you people of the land, / says the LORD, and work! /
For I am with you, says the LORD of hosts.*
—HAGGAI 2:4

The philosophy of work in Catholic social thought is simply breathtaking. The Church teaches that work was given to Adam and Eve before the Fall; "it is therefore not a punishment or curse." Furthermore, "work represents a fundamental dimension of human existence as participation not only in the act of creation, but also in that of redemption." If you struggle with your work, study precisely what the Church teaches and be refreshed and reformed in your relationship to your labor.

Haggai 2:1–9
Psalm 43
Luke 9:18–22

SEPTEMBER 28

See, I am coming to dwell among you, says the LORD.
—ZECHARIAH 2:15

It is striking to note just how manifestly the Old Testament points to the New. See just how relentlessly Scripture upholds this notion: God is with us, dwelling among us, near to us, interested in us in a particular way. I cannot escape how pointed this message is. How is this made manifest in my life?

Zechariah 2:5–9, 14–15
Jeremiah 31:10–13
Luke 9:43b–45

SEPTEMBER 29

*You, man of God, pursue righteousness, devotion, faith, love, patience,
and gentleness.*
—1 TIMOTHY 6:11

Righteousness, devotion, faith, love, patience, gentleness:
O Lord, make this the litany of my day and my life.

Amos 6:1a, 4–7
Psalm 146
1 Timothy 6:11–16
Luke 16:19–31

Thus says the LORD of hosts: / Lo, I will rescue my people . . . / I will bring them back to dwell within Jerusalem. / They shall be my people, and I will be their God, / with faithfulness and justice.
—ZECHARIAH 8:8

St. Jerome has been attributed with this idea: "Ignorance of the Scriptures is ignorance of Christ." What ignorance does this verse from Zechariah dispel? That God has abandoned me, is faithless, unjust, disinterested? That I am not worth saving? That God would never claim me for his own?

Zechariah 8:1–8
Psalm 102
Luke 9:46–50

Tuesday

OCTOBER 1

• ST. THÉRÈSE OF THE CHILD JESUS, VIRGIN AND DOCTOR
OF THE CHURCH •

He resolutely determined to journey to Jerusalem.
—LUKE 9:51

Fully aware of what awaits him, Jesus remains "resolutely determined." St. Thérèse in her "little way" is also resolutely determined. She writes, "Great deeds are forbidden me. The only way I can prove my love is by scattering flowers and these flowers are every little sacrifice, every glance and word, and the doing of the least actions for love." Though the outward character of these sacrifices—the crucifixion and the "little way"—are different, the resolution is the same. To grow in love is a crucifixion, or many little crucifixions, along the way to Jerusalem.

Zechariah 8:20–23
Psalm 87
Luke 9:51–56

OCTOBER 2

· THE HOLY GUARDIAN ANGELS ·

For he will command his angels concerning you to guard you in all your ways.
—PSALM 91:11

Angels are always in the thick of things: the Annunciation, the birth of Christ, tending Jesus in the desert, announcing the plan of heaven, protecting, guarding, guiding. They intercede for us before the face of God. Our Father in heaven has ordered the world such that it is full to the brim of such beautiful, holy creatures. How generous.

Holy angels, pray for us.

Exodus 23:20–23
Psalm 91
Matthew 18:1–5, 10

OCTOBER 3

The harvest is abundant but the laborers are few; so ask the master of the
harvest to send out laborers for his harvest.
—LUKE 10:2

You are the harvest.

You are the wheat.

Would the Lord entrust you to just anyone?

Lord, you are generous. Send us more men and women who
will delight in serving you, gathering up the Church with
singleness of purpose.

Nehemiah 8:1–4a, 5–6, 7b–12
Psalm 19
Luke 10:1–12

Friday

OCTOBER 4

• ST. FRANCIS OF ASSISI •

O LORD, my allotted portion and my cup,
you it is who hold fast my lot.
—PSALM 16:5

As far as we know, St. Francis was the first to receive the
stigmata. Not many people receive such a sign of holiness.
Still, we are invited to bear the holy wounds of Jesus on our
hearts and minds. How? By accepting and even being
grateful for whatever sufferings we experience, and by
asking God to redeem us through them, to make full use of
them to in ways that only heaven can.

Galatians 6:14–18
Psalm 16
Matthew 11:25–30

≥ 307 ≤

*Fear not, my children; call out to God! / He who brought this upon you
will remember you. / As your hearts have been disposed to stray from
God, / turn now ten times the more to seek him; / For he who has brought
disaster upon you will, / in saving you, bring you back enduring joy.*
—BARUCH 4:27–29

It is never too late to turn your heart back to God and to
enter his plan for you, that of deep and abiding joy.

Baruch 4:5–12, 27–29
Psalm 69
Luke 10:17–24

OCTOBER 6

For the vision still has its time, / presses on to fulfillment, and will not disappoint; / if it delays, wait for it, / it will surely come, it will not be late.
—HABAKKUK 2:3

We wait for Jesus. We pray and beg and pour out our hearts, and impossibly he says, "Wait, child. I will not be late. My timing is perfect. My fulfillment of every promise is satisfying beyond measure. You will know such joy! Child, I am coming. I will not be late."

May we grow in the virtues of patience and holy poise.

Habakkuk 1:2–3; 2:2–4
Psalm 95
2 Timothy 1:6–8, 13–14
Luke 17:5–10

From the belly of the fish Jonah prayed to the LORD, his God. Then the
LORD commanded the fish to spew Jonah upon the shore.
—JONAH 2:1, 10

Poor fleeing Jonah, spewed up onshore by a sea creature.
The source of our rescue may not always be as glamorous as
we wish, but our rescue comes nonetheless. Mary teaches
us this paradox, too: her queenship lies in her humility. Her
tremendous interceding power issues from meekness and
quiet courage.

Our Lady of the Rosary, pray for us who sometimes try to
flee from God's way and will.

Jonah 1:1–2; 2:1,11
Jonah 2:3–8
Luke 10:25–37

OCTOBER 8

The word of the LORD came to Jonah a second time: "Set out for the great city of Nineveh, and announce to it the message that I will tell you." So Jonah made ready and went to Nineveh, according to the LORD's bidding.
—JONAH 3:1–3

Our God is a God of endless second chances.

We praise you, Lord, for your unending patience and mercy. Grant us the grace always to take up our second chances when we have fearfully passed over the first.

Jonah 3:1–10
Psalm 130
Luke 10:38–42

OCTOBER 9

"Lord, teach us to pray."
—LUKE 11:1

What are the disciples really asking? What are they really longing for in their query to Jesus? St. Pius said, "One looks for God in books, but finds Him in prayer." Here the disciples are not looking for a treatise or an academic lesson. They are not even asking for guidance as much as they are looking for communion and connection, the most effective means to relationship with the loving will of the Father.

Jonah 4:1–11
Psalm 86
Luke 11:1–4

OCTOBER 10

*For you who fear my name, there will arise
the sun of justice with its healing rays.*
—MALACHI 3:20

When I lived in Alaska, the returning sun of spring took on
a special significance after the long, dark winter. You craved
sunshine; you thirsted for it deep in your bones. The spring
sun of Alaska was healing indeed. In those dark winters of
the spirit, we remember that spring is coming with its
healing warmth and light, to bring about new things, green
and growing things, deep in the heart of humankind.

Malachi 3:13–20
Psalm 1
Luke 11:5–13

OCTOBER 11

Whoever does not gather with me scatters.
—LUKE 11:23

We are a wildly unrecollected, ungathered people. Some of the more subtle forms of sin take on this scattering quality. Distraction, disruption, interruption, and breaking apart—especially in its less obvious forms—can be deadly for the soul of the human family. Jesus was always interested in gathering us up together to build the entire Church body in all its rich multiplicity.

Today I will spend some time remembering the ways in which Jesus calls us to unity.

Joel 1:13–15; 2:1–2
Psalm 9
Luke 11:15–26

OCTOBER 12

*Apply the sickle,
for the harvest is ripe.*
—JOEL 4:13

Note that harvest involves cutting. Note also that ripening
is a fulfillment, not an end.

We are brought to the table of the Lord when we are ripe
with holiness.

Joel 4:12–21
Psalm 97
Luke 11:27–28

⋑ 315 ⋐

OCTOBER 13

The word of God is not chained.
—2 TIMOTHY 2:9

The word of God is not bound or imprisoned in any way.
Already it has reached the four corners of the earth and
shall continue its journey, gathering up the faithful, filling
the hearts of those who are unloved, and pouring itself into
the ear that hears. The word of God will have the world.

2 Kings 5:14–17
Psalm 98
2 Timothy 2:8–13
Luke 17:11–19

There is something greater than Jonah here.
—LUKE 11:32

Jonah's greatness was located in how God used him to convert hardened hearts. Unlike Jonah, Jesus moved toward the fulfillment of God's word—his passion, death, and resurrection—willingly and wholeheartedly. He needed no cajoling. The miracles he performed along the way were not sideshow acts for sensationalists but evidence of his saving, healing power. Still, this will not be enough for some. The Resurrection will not be enough for some. Forgiveness will not be enough for some.

Romans 1:1–7
Psalm 98
Luke 11:29–32

Ever since the creation of the world, his invisible attributes of eternal power and divinity have been able to be understood and perceived in what he has made.
—ROMANS 1:20

Teresa of Ávila said it this way:

Christ has no body now, but yours. No hands, no feet on earth, but yours.

Yours are the eyes through which Christ looks upon the world with compassion.

Yours are the feet with which Christ walks to do good.

Yours are the hands with which Christ blesses the world.

Romans 1:16–25
Psalm 19
Luke 11:37–41

⇒ 318 ⇐

OCTOBER 16

God . . . will repay everyone according to his works, eternal life to those who seek glory, honor and immortality through perseverance in good works, but wrath and fury to those who selfishly disobey the truth and obey wickedness.
—ROMANS 2:7–8

We do choose our lives. Of course we don't choose some things, such as car crashes and illness and every kind of difficulty, but we do choose how we will respond to the things that happen to us, the circumstances into which we are born, and the way we move through the world.
We choose.

Romans 2:1–11
Psalm 62
Luke 11:42–46

My soul waits for the LORD
more than sentinels wait for the dawn.
—PSALM 130:6

Sentinels stand guard looking for the enemy, often at points
of passage, points of importance. The sentinel on guard
throughout the night has limited vision, making his work
even more perilous and difficult. He stands in constant
strain. Dawn comes as a sweet relief from his labors, from
darkness and limited vision.

Lord, bring your dawn of light and clarity of heart.

Romans 3:21–30
Psalm 130
Luke 11:47–54

"Go on your way; behold, I am sending you like lambs among wolves."
—LUKE 10:3

The truth is hard sometimes, and Jesus knew it. He never hides the danger of his evangelizing work from us; in fact, he is upfront about what the Christian life will entail with respect to suffering and martyrdom. When persecution confronts us—as individuals or as a Church—we take consolation in Christ's knowledge of our suffering. He anticipated it, prepared us for it—and will ultimately conquer it. Jesus isn't surprised by persecution, and he will never leave us to suffer it without him.

2 Timothy 4:9–17b
Psalm 145
Luke 10:1–9

He believed, hoping against hope that he would become "the father of many nations," according to what was said, "Thus shall your descendants be."
—ROMANS 4:18

Abraham's faith is held up for us: hope against hope, Paul calls it. This childless man becomes the father of many nations.

In what area of my life do I need to borrow the faith of Abraham, this hope against hope?

Romans 4:13, 16–18
Psalm 105
Luke 12:8–12

All Scripture is inspired by God . . . so that one who belongs to God
may be competent, equipped for every good work.
—2 TIMOTHY 3:16–17

You have everything you need to do all that God would
have you do. He is interested in your competence, your
preparation, and your being well-equipped to do what he
asks. And where you lack, he will make up for your
deficiency.

Exodus 17:8–13
Psalm 121
2 Timothy 3:14—4:2
Luke 18:1–8

⇒ 323 ⇐

OCTOBER 21

"Take care to guard against all greed, for though one may be rich, one's life does not consist of possessions."
—LUKE 12:15

More than avoiding greed, many of the great spiritual masters encourage us "to experience the abiding instability of one who possesses nothing." Carlo Carretto writes, "We must learn to accept instability, put ourselves every now and then in the condition of having to say, 'Give us this day our daily bread,' with real anxiety because the larder is empty . . . keep open in the wall of the soul the great window of living faith in the Providence of an all-powerful God."

Romans 4:20–25
Luke 1:69–75
Luke 12:13–21

Just as through one transgression condemnation came upon all, so, through one righteous act acquittal and life came to all. For just as through the disobedience of one man the many were made sinners, so, through the obedience of the one the many will be made righteous.
—ROMANS 5:21

We participate in undoing human transgression. Léon Bloy writes, "Every man who performs a free act projects his personality into infinity. If he gives from his feeble heart a penny to a poor man, that penny pierces the hand of the poor, falls, breaks through the earth, pierces the sun, transverses the firmament, and captures the universe. . . . It heals the sick, consoles the hopeless, calms storms, redeems captives, converts the infidel, and protects the human race."

Romans 5:12, 15b, 17–19, 20b–21
Psalm 40
Luke 12:35–38

Sin is not to have any power over you, since you are not under the law but under grace.
—ROMANS 6:14

What sin has power over you? Do you gossip? Are you overly critical? Is it difficult to share your resources with those who need them? Do you lie, drink too much, spend too much, work too much? Are you addicted? Does your sin cause you to despair? The grace of Christ is more powerful than any sin, than all sin put together. You need only turn to grace, ask for it, invite it, accept it. Let grace have its way with you.

Romans 6:12–18
Psalm 124
Luke 12:39–48

OCTOBER 24

*The wages of sin is death, but the gift of God is eternal life in
Christ Jesus.*
—ROMANS 6:23

Sin equals death. I die a hundred little deaths every day: the
mean thought, the petty vanities, the critical eye, the tiny
lies I tell myself about how this or that really isn't that bad.
But then I go to Mass, go to confession, make amends, say a
prayer, say a hundred prayers, ask God for help, for light,
for life—and he comes streaming in, burning up all that
death inside me. Pouring in his life.

Romans 6:19–23
Psalm 1
Luke 12:49–53

⇒ 327 ⇐

OCTOBER 25

*I do not do the good I want, but I do the evil I do not want. . . . I take
delight in the law of God in my inner self, but I see in my members
another principle at war with the law of my mind, taking me captive to
the law of sin.*
—ROMANS 7:19, 22

I am at war! My inner self is doing battle to free me from sin
and to release me to the law of God. But I am not alone in
this war. It's a war God wants me to win. Jesus will deliver
me from this mortal coil if I ask and ask and ask again.

Romans 7:18–25
Psalm 119
Luke 12:54–59

OCTOBER 26

"I shall cultivate the ground around [this fig tree] and fertilize it; it may bear fruit in the future."
—LUKE 13:8

Sometimes all we need is a little fertilizer, a little cultivation. Sometimes those around us need a second chance, a little more time, and a little more attention. It is a sign of hope to believe that one day they may bear fruit and that one day I may be more fruitful than I am now.

Romans 8:1–11
Psalm 24
Luke 13:1–9

OCTOBER 27

The prayer of the lowly pierces the clouds;
it does not rest till it reaches its goal.
—SIRACH 35:17

Are you imagining that you are not heard? That you are not dazzling enough, powerful enough, exalted enough? That God is somehow wooed by the wealthy, the powerful, and the exalted of this world?

What does it mean to be lowly?

What is the power of humility?

Sirach 35:12–14, 16–18
Psalm 34
2 Timothy 4:6–8, 16–18
Luke 18:9–14

You are fellow citizens with the holy ones and members of the household of God, built upon the foundation of the Apostles and prophets, with Christ Jesus himself as the capstone. Through him the whole structure is held together.
—EPHESIANS 2:20–21

The chaos of the world is no measure of the truest part of you. You belong to God. Though things may feel as if they are falling apart, remember who holds you together. Remember that you are part of a spiritual household that cannot be destroyed. It cannot be brought down Remember who holds together the family of God.

Ephesians 2:19–22
Psalm 19
Luke 6:12–16

OCTOBER 29

Jesus said, "What is the Kingdom of God like? To what can I compare it? . . . It is like yeast that a woman took and mixed in with three measures of wheat flour until the whole batch of dough was leavened."
—LUKE 13:20–21

The primary property of yeast is to expand and make fuller, to enliven and leaven and raise up.

The primary purpose of the Kingdom of God is to bring us into more life, eternal life, to raise us up and enliven our hearts toward real things.

Romans 8:18–25
Psalm 126
Luke 13:18–21

The Spirit comes to the aid of our weakness; for we do not know how to pray as we ought, but the Spirit himself intercedes with inexpressible groanings.
—ROMANS 8:26

The Spirit can and does, shall we say, finish those sentences the heart speaks.

Romans 8:26–30
Psalm 13
Luke 13:22–30

⇒ 333 ⇐

OCTOBER 31

*What will separate us from the love of Christ? Will anguish, or distress,
or persecution, or famine, or nakedness, or peril, or the sword?*
—ROMANS 8:35

Will governments, or disease, or rejection, or betrayal
separate me from the love of Christ? Will the media or the
opinions of others ever have so much power that the love
of Christ cannot reach me?

Romans 8:31b–39
Psalm 109
Luke 13:31–35

I had a vision of a great multitude, which no one could count, from every nation, race, people, and tongue. They stood before the throne and before the Lamb, wearing white robes and holding palm branches in their hands. They cried out in a loud voice:
"Salvation comes from our God."
—REVELATION 7:9–10

G. K. Chesterton wrote, "The saint is medicine because he is an antidote. Indeed that is why the saint is often a martyr; he was mistaken for a poison because he is an antidote. He will generally be found restoring the world to sanity by exaggerating whatever the world neglects . . .'Ye are salt of the earth.' Salt seasons and preserves beef, not because it is like beef; but because it's very unlike it."

Revelation 7:2–4, 9–14
Psalm 24
1 John 3:1–3
Matthew 5:1–12a

• THE COMMEMORATION OF ALL THE FAITHFUL DEPARTED
(ALL SOULS' DAY) •

I believe that I shall see the bounty of the LORD
in the land of the living.
—PSALM 27:13

The monks used to pray: *memento mori*, keep your death in
mind. We do not pray for the dead or meditate on our own
deaths out of some macabre obsession with suffering but to
place our lives in the greater context of reality—that is,
eternity. Adrienne von Speyr writes, "The believer may not
approach the tasks of his life here below solely with earthly
considerations. . . . For he is a citizen of heaven, and his
citizenship is one of love."

Isaiah 25:6, 7–9
Psalm 27
Romans 6:3–9
Matthew 25:31–46
or other readings

NOVEMBER 3

*For you love all things that are / and loathe nothing that you have
made, / for what you hated, you would not have fashioned. / And how
could a thing remain, unless you willed it; / or be preserved, had it not
been called forth by you?*
—WISDOM 11:24–25

It is good that you exist. By the very breath of God, you
have been called forth into existence, given a unique and
exalted place in all that is. You are preserved in love for all
eternity. It is good—eternally good, immeasurably
good—that you are. You are loved beyond measure by one
whose love knows no bounds.

Wisdom 11:22—12:1
Psalm 145
2 Thessalonians 1:11—2:2
Luke 19:1–10

For from him and through him and for him are all things.
—ROMANS 11:36

Is Jesus truly the center of my life? How can I invite him
more and more to reside in the place only he can fill?

Romans 11:29–36
Psalm 69
Luke 14:12–14

NOVEMBER 5

Rejoice with those who rejoice, weep with those who weep.
—ROMANS 12:15

It is a great existential need of the human spirit to be
affirmed in every aspect of who and what we are, and to
make our experiences real and meaningful, we must share
them with others. We show great mercy and tenderness
when we are able to be truly joyful with others, without
jealousy or envy, and when we can be sorrowful with them
as well, sharing their burdens, showing tenderness and
compassion.

Romans 12:5–16ab
Psalm 131
Luke 14:15–24

"Everyone of you who does not renounce all his possessions cannot be my disciple."
—LUKE 14:33

When I read this, do I automatically tense, recoil just a little bit, rescind just a smidge? If I am in love, there is nothing I would hold back from my beloved. Maybe the problem here is not that I am greedy or grasping; maybe the problem is that I lack love.

Romans 13:8–10
Psalm 112
Luke 14:25–33

NOVEMBER 7

"There will be more joy in heaven over one sinner who repents than over ninety-nine righteous people who have no need of repentance."
—LUKE 15:7

What of the ninety-nine sheep left behind? It would have been rare for a shepherd to leave his flock unattended. If a sheep wandered off, the head shepherd would go in search of it, leaving the rest of the flock well-attended by other shepherds. The point is not that Jesus loves sinners more—we're all sinners—but that he would leave behind not even one of us. He's not driven by a majority vote; Jesus is interested in the conversion of every single, solitary one of us.

Romans 14:7–12
Psalm 27
Luke 15:1–10

I have written to you rather boldly in some respects to remind you,
because of the grace given me by God to be a minister of Christ Jesus . . .
in performing the priestly service of the Gospel of God.
—ROMANS 15:15

When my brother was ordained, the difference was palpable. He'd been given a confidence through his ordination, and it was apparent immediately. But this confidence was not in himself; it was in God. We all have access to this kind of priestly confidence, this in-filling of the Holy Spirit respective to our vocations. Each of us can move boldly in God's appointments for us. Today, be bold for Jesus; be bold in love.

Romans 15:14–21
Psalm 98
Luke 16:1–8

He made a whip out of cords and drove them all out of the temple area, with the sheep and oxen, and spilled the coins of the money-changers and overturned their tables, and to those who sold doves he said, "Take these out of here, and stop making my Father's house a marketplace." His disciples recalled the words of Scripture, "Zeal for your house will consume me."
—JOHN 2:15–17

Jesus, meek and mild: he is the Lamb, the Beloved Son. We must never imagine that he was powerless or afraid to fight. But the Father's will is mystery that includes a time to turn tables and a time to carry the cross.

We pray for your wisdom, Lord, and your zeal.

Ezekiel 47:1–2, 8–9, 12
Psalm 46
1 Corinthians 3:9c–11, 16–17
John 2:13–22

NOVEMBER 10

*May our Lord Jesus Christ himself and God our Father . . . encourage
your hearts and strengthen them in every good deed and word.*
—2 THESSALONIANS 2:16

Pope Leo the Great is probably best known for his
declaration and defense of petrine supremacy, that is, the
office of the pope as head of the Church. It's a tough role.
Today let us offer this prayer for the pope and all Church
leaders—that they be encouraged in heart and
strengthened through the grace of God in every word
and deed.

2 Maccabees 7:1–2, 9–14
Psalm 17
2 Thessalonians 2:16—3:5
Luke 20:27–38 or 20:27, 34–38

For wisdom is a kindly spirit.
—WISDOM 1:6

Why shouldn't wisdom be kind? What has she to fear? The wise one knows: we are created for eternity. The wise one knows: Christ will redeem those who turn to him. The wise one knows: Jesus will have the last word. The wise one understands: there's nothing anyone can do to my body, mind, bank account, reputation, or safety that will keep me from the love of Christ.

Wisdom 1:1–7
Psalm 139
Luke 17:1–6

Those who trust in him shall understand truth,
and the faithful shall abide with him in love:
Because grace and mercy are with his holy ones, / and his care is with
his elect.
—WISDOM 3:9

Truth and love, grace and mercy—these are the things that grow up around God's faithful. These are the great gifts of God's care.

Wisdom 2:23—3:9
Psalm 34
Luke 17:7–10

⇒346⇐

One of them, realizing he had been healed, returned, glorifying God in a loud voice; and he fell at the feet of Jesus and thanked him. . . . Jesus said in reply, "Ten were cleansed, were they not? Where are the other nine?"
—LUKE 17:15–17

Lord, let me be among those who fall at your feet and thank you. Your healing is real within me; your blessing, abundant; your mercy, enduring.

Wisdom 6:1–11
Psalm 82
Luke 17:11–19

Thursday

NOVEMBER 14

*She is fairer than the sun
and surpasses every constellation of the stars.*
—WISDOM 7:29

How does one become more beautiful?

By becoming wiser.

Jesus, make me fairer than the sun, a true beauty, your
dazzling wise one.

Wisdom 7:22—8:1
Psalm 119
Luke 17:20–25

⇒ 348 ⇐

For from the greatness and the beauty of created things
their original author, by analogy, is seen.
—WISDOM 13:5

Hans Urs von Balthasar explains that "Every experience of beauty points to infinity." He writes that "Beauty dances as an uncontained splendor around the double constellation of the true and the good. . . . she will not allow herself to be separated and banned from her two sisters without taking them along with herself in an act of mysterious vengeance. We can be sure that whoever sneers at her name can no longer pray and soon will no longer be able to love."

Wisdom 13:1–9
Psalm 19
Luke 17:26–37

"Because this widow keeps bothering me I shall deliver a just decision . . ." The Lord said, "Pay attention to what the dishonest judge says. Will not God then secure the rights of his chosen ones who call out to him day and night?"
—LUKE 18:5–7

Does God love a squeaky wheel? We don't persist in prayer because we believe God's a bad listener or doesn't want to deal with us. Rather, we persist because we hope and because we have faith in God's generous heart.

Wisdom 18:14–16; 19:6–9
Psalm 105
Luke 18:1–8

NOVEMBER 17

We instructed you that if anyone was unwilling to work, neither should that one eat.
—2 THESSALONIANS 3:10

Idleness is simply another way to be greedy. We are designed for work, as is clear even from the Creation narratives. Work is a way by which we participate in the life of God and further show our devotion. My father got up every day for more than fifty years and put on a suit and went off to a very difficult job, one that put seven children through college and launched us on our way. Thank you, Dad.

Malachi 3:19–20
Psalm 98
2 Thessalonians 3:7–12
Luke 21:5–19

"Jesus, Son of David, have pity on me!"
—LUKE 18:38

When the blind man calls out to Jesus, people rebuke him,
but he simply cries out all the more. Sometimes the world
would like to tell us we are crazy for crying out to God;
we're a nuisance, something to be shushed into submission.
At such times we can recall Jesus' response to this man:
"What do you want me to do for you?" The blind man's
vision is restored immediately. Sometimes we do have to
ask loudly above the din around us and remember that Jesus
is here to encounter us personally, eye-to-eye.

1 Maccabees 1:10–15, 41–43, 54–57, 62–63
Psalm 119
Luke 18:35–43

NOVEMBER 19

When he was about to die under the blows, [Eleazar] groaned and said: "The Lord in his holy knowledge knows full well that, although I could have escaped death, I am not only enduring terrible pain in my body from this scourging, but also suffering it with joy in my soul because of my devotion to him." This is how he died, leaving in his death a model of courage and an unforgettable example of virtue not only for the young but for the whole nation.
—2 MACCABEES 6:30–31

Lord, I pray for the grace of a holy death.

2 Maccabees 6:18–31
Psalm 3
Luke 19:1–10

NOVEMBER 20

"I beg you, child, to look at the heavens and the earth and see all that is in them; then you will know that God did not make them out of existing things; and in the same way the human race came into existence. Do not be afraid of this executioner, but be worthy of your brothers and accept death, so that in the time of mercy I may receive you again with them."
—2 MACCABEES 7:28–29

What courage! The mother of Maccabees is an extraordinary woman. Here we see heroic parenting, mothering that exhorts a child toward heaven and not toward her own agenda. Such mothering must mirror the fathering Jesus received.

2 Maccabees 7:1, 20–31
Psalm 17
Luke 19:11–28

NOVEMBER 21

• THE PRESENTATION OF THE BLESSED VIRGIN MARY •

Perfect in beauty,
God shines forth.
—PSALM 50:2

Beauty is one of the great languages of heaven. But do we know how to speak it anymore? Pope Benedict XVI writes that "to disdain or to reject the impact produced by the response of the heart in the encounter with beauty as a true form of knowledge would impoverish us and dry up our faith and our theology. We must rediscover this form of knowledge; it is a pressing need of our time."

Lord, in this day, may I see your beauty.

1 Maccabees 2:15–29
Psalm 50
Luke 9:41–44

"My house shall be a house of prayer, but you have made it a den of thieves."
—LUKE 19:46

It is good to be reminded that corruption can creep into even the holiest parts of our lives. Sometimes the places we least expect or the places we are most likely to protect can become vulnerable to deception and decay.

Today I will keep my spiritual house a house of prayer, one that constantly seeks communion with heaven.

1 Maccabees 4:36–37, 52–59
1 Chronicles 29:10–12
Luke 19:45–48

NOVEMBER 23

I will give thanks to you, O LORD, with all my heart.
—PSALM 9:2

Note how often the whole heart is referenced in Scripture.
This implies that nothing is held back, that no part is
hidden or kept to oneself. Are there parts of me I am trying
to hide and control? Are there aspects of my life for which I
resist God's healing touch?

1 Maccabees 6:1–13
Psalm 9
Luke 20:27–40

⇒ 357 ⇐

He is the image of the invisible God, / the firstborn of all creation. / For in him were created all things in heaven and on earth, / the visible and the invisible. . . . / all things were created through him and for him. / He is before all things, / and in him all things hold together.
—1 COLOSSIANS 1:15–17

This passage is saying, as Carlo Carretto notes, that "the whole man must be transformed by the Gospel message. Nothing he does can be indifferent. All his actions must be determined by the Gospel."

Lord, I wish to hold back no aspect of myself. May you, king of heaven and earth, move through me, before me, around me, seen and unseen.

2 Samuel 5:1–3
Psalm 122
Colossians 1:12–20
Luke 23:35–43

He noticed a poor widow putting in two small coins. He said, " . . . this poor widow put in more than all the rest; for those others have all made offerings from their surplus wealth, but she, from her poverty, has offered her whole livelihood."
—LUKE 21:3–4

Jesus asks us to give, not from our surplus, but from our poverty. This is true not only in our worldly goods, but also in our spiritual poverty. Where am I poorest? In my lack of faith or charity? I can make an offering of this as well.

Daniel 1:1–6, 8–20
Daniel 3:52–56
Luke 21:1–4

NOVEMBER 26

The God of heaven will set up a kingdom that shall never be destroyed or delivered up to another people; rather, it shall break in pieces all these kingdoms and put an end to them, and it shall stand forever.
—DANIEL 2:44

The Old and New Testaments find their fullness in their complementarity. It can be helpful when we are meditating on the Old Testament to ask ourselves, *where do we find Jesus in this passage?* And when we do, his presence rises to the surface of the page and strengthens our understanding and our hope.

Daniel 2:31–45
Daniel 3:57–61
Luke 21:5–11

NOVEMBER 27

Sun and moon, bless the Lord . . .
Stars of heaven, bless the Lord . . .
Every shower and dew, bless the Lord . . .
All you winds, bless the Lord . . .
Fire and heat, bless the Lord . . .
Cold and chill, bless the Lord . . .
—DANIEL 3:62–67

This canticle is frequently prayed in the Office of daily prayer. I have prayed it many times with the seminarians in my brother's class. One early morning I ran into Nate, who held up his coffee mug and said with a beautiful, broad smile, "Coffee and cream, bless the Lord!" Even in the little things, "Praise and exalt him forever."

Daniel 5:1–6, 13–14, 16–17, 23–28
Daniel 3:62–67
Luke 21:12–19

NOVEMBER 28

• THANKSGIVING •

"Blessed be the LORD who has given rest to his people Israel, just as he promised. Not a single word has gone unfulfilled of the entire generous promise he made through his servant Moses."
—1 KINGS 8:56

God keeps his promises. So what has he promised us? Wealth, health, and wisdom? Protection from worldly dangers, loneliness, and economic decline? The promise is eternal life; the promise is that God will remember us when we come into his kingdom and that he leaves with us the Advocate to help us get there.

1 Kings 8:55–61
Psalm 138
Colossians 3:12–17
Luke 17:11–19

NOVEMBER 29

*His dominion is an everlasting dominion
that shall not be taken away,
his kingship shall not be destroyed.*
—DANIEL 7:14

Some things are steadfast and reliable: the sun, the moon,
the stars in the heavens, gravity, waves on the ocean, the
turning of tides, the presence of angels. Also time, all of
your hours, minutes, and seconds moving into the present
moment never to be repeated. God's dominion is surer than
these. His kingship will outlast all. Live in and rest in his
absolute dominion.

Daniel 7:2–14
Daniel 3:75–81
Luke 21:29–33

At once they left their nets and followed him.
—MATTHEW 4:20

Lord, give me an attentive ear and an obedient heart, one
that hears you clearly. I want to have the same fervor as the
first apostles, to literally drop what I'm doing—my
livelihood, my whole life—to follow you.

Romans 10:9–18
Psalm 19
Matthew 4:18–22

DECEMBER 1

It is the hour now for you to awake from sleep.
—ROMANS 13:11

In this dawn of Advent, Lord, awaken my spirit to every gentle stirring of grace, mercy, innocence, and peace you shower over me.

Isaiah 2:1–5
Psalm 122
Romans 13:11–14
Matthew 24:37–44

DECEMBER 2

"Only say the word and my servant will be healed."
—MATTHEW 8:8

We echo the words of the centurion at every Mass: *only say
the word and I shall be healed.* May we echo his faith as well, a
faith that caused Jesus to say, "In no one in Israel have I
found such faith." I wonder if the source of his amazement
was this centurion's understanding of and deep respect for
authority.

The next time I utter this prayer, I will remember the
centurion and his tremendous faith in the authority of Jesus.

Isaiah 4:2–6
Psalm 122
Matthew 8:5–11

DECEMBER 3

• ST. FRANCIS XAVIER, PRIEST •

"Although you have hidden these things from the wise and the learned you have revealed them to the childlike."
—LUKE 10:21

I met Cecilia when she was two. About the only thing I recall of our first acquaintance was that she cried when I picked up her infant sister. But her parents report that for some time after that, Ce prayed for me daily, spontaneously. Every time a siren passed and the family prayed for the first responders and any injured, Ce would add, "And Liz Kelly." Since they lived near a fire station, I was prayed for as many as five times a day. No doubt, Ce recognized something hidden even from me.

Isaiah 11:1–10
Psalm 72
Luke 10:21–24

Wednesday

DECEMBER 4

• ST. JOHN DAMASCENE, PRIEST AND DOCTOR OF THE CHURCH •

*The LORD will wipe away
the tears from all faces.*
—ISAIAH 25:8

This is part of Advent's great promise: the great tenderness
Jesus offers us. Eye to eye, heart to heart, he holds each one
of us, precious and dear, and the sorrow he wipes from our
faces is more than just the difficulties of life, but the sorrow
brought by our sins, the million ways we have rejected
God's good gifts.

Isaiah 25:6–10
Psalm 23
Matthew 15:29–37

DECEMBER 5

Trust in the LORD forever!
For the LORD is an eternal Rock.
—ISAIAH 26:4

Sometimes the bottom drops out, things fall apart, the center doesn't hold—but that's only in the temporal order, this life that has yet to be fully born into eternal things. Somehow I know, believe, and understand that in heaven, things hold together. In God, all things work together for good. That I cannot comprehend forever does not negate its existence nor its power and presence active in my life.

Isaiah 26:1–6
Psalm 118
Matthew 7:21, 24–27

DECEMBER 6

• ST. NICHOLAS, BISHOP •

One thing I ask of the LORD;
this I seek;
To dwell in the house of the LORD all the days of my life,
That I may gaze on the loveliness of the LORD
and contemplate his temple.
—PSALM 27:4

Frederica Mathewes-Green suggests that if you want more
beautiful eyes, you might pray more. Yes, and if you want a
more beautiful spirit, say thank-you continually—it is the
means of gazing on the loveliness of the Lord; it is actively
contemplating his temple.

Isaiah 29:17–24
Psalm 27
Matthew 9:27–31

DECEMBER 7

• ST. AMBROSE, BISHOP AND DOCTOR OF THE CHURCH •

O people of Zion . . .
no more will you weep;
He will be gracious to you when you cry out,
as soon as he hears he will answer you.
The LORD will give you the bread you need
and the water for which you thirst.
No longer will your Teacher hide himself,
but with your own eyes you shall see your Teacher,
While from behind, a voice shall sound in your ears;
"This is the way; walk in it."
—ISAIAH 30:19–20

If I struggle to know the will of God, it might help to ask if
my own agenda is keeping it hidden.

Isaiah 30:19–21, 23–26
Psalm 147
Matthew 9:35—10:1,5a, 6–8

DECEMBER 8

With a little child to guide them.
—ISAIAH 11:6

After my eight-year-old nephew's first confession, my sister reports that he sat down in the pew and said with much relief, "Whew, I have a clean soul!"

Indeed.

Isaiah 11:1–10
Psalm 72
Romans 15:4–9
Matthew 3:1–12

He chose us in him, before the foundation of the world, to be holy and without blemish before him.
—EPHESIANS 1:4

Everything in Mary's life points to the truth of Christ. His birthing in the world required an extraordinary act of grace—the immaculate conception of his mother—hidden and quiet and unknown to the world, as are so many of the holiest things.

Lord, let me be without blemish before you, even in the most hidden and quiet places of my person.

Genesis 3:9–15, 20
Psalm 98
Ephesians 1:3–6, 11–12
Luke 1:26–38

DECEMBER 10

Like a shepherd he feeds his flock;
in his arms he gathers the lambs,
Carrying them in his bosom,
and leading the ewes with care.
—ISAIAH 40:11

In word and deed, in reality and eternity, God cares for us.
He carries us always near the heart, draws those who are
humble and vulnerable ever deeper into his care.

Isaiah 40:1–11
Psalm 96
Matthew 18:12–14

DECEMBER 11

• ST. DAMASUS I, POPE •

They that hope in the LORD will renew their strength,
they will soar as with eagles' wings;
They will run and not grow weary,
walk and not grow faint.
—ISAIAH 40:31

In the shadows of this world, the hope-light of Advent spills out to illuminate even the darkest, most despairing human corners. Who around me needs hope? Who around me has grown weary, faint with despair? Who needs to borrow my hope until it becomes their own? Who needs me to hold the lamp for them?

Isaiah 40:25–31
Psalm 103
Matthew 11:28–30

DECEMBER 12

Mary said to the angel, "How can this be?"
—LUKE 1:34

It may be one of the most common prayers ever launched
heavenward by the human race. Before the extraordinary
blessing of God, we stand dazed and disbelieving.
Wonderment is only natural in the presence of grace.

Zechariah 2:14–17 or Revelation 11:19a; 12:1a–6ab, 10
Judith 13
Luke 1:26–38 or 1:39–47

DECEMBER 13

• ST. LUCY, VIRGIN AND MARTYR •

I, the LORD, your God,
teach you what is for your good,
and lead you on the way you should go.
—ISAIAH 48:17

We can know the truth. We can know the way ahead. There are times when the way ahead is clear, when what is for our good is obvious. Those who would try to obfuscate the spiritual life may not understand the difference between mystery and obscurity, between confusion and discernment, between mercy and insecurity, between paradoxical truth and pure contradiction.

Lord, give us clarity of heart and mind.

Isaiah 48:17–19
Psalm 1
Matthew 11:16–19

DECEMBER 14

• ST. JOHN OF THE CROSS, PRIEST AND DOCTOR OF THE CHURCH •

"So also will the Son of Man suffer at their hands."
—MATTHEW 17:12

It is a common human flaw to distrust, hate, and abuse the very thing that will save us. John of the Cross was beaten and imprisoned by his confreres, the very people he sought to help and love and encourage in the reform of the Carmelites. He must have understood in a unique way the sufferings of Christ, who came to love and restore us and bring us to heaven—and who suffers at our hands.

Sirach 48:1–4, 9–11
Psalm 80
Matthew 17:9a, 10–13

See how the farmer waits for the precious fruit of the earth, being patient with it until it receives the early and the late rains. You too must be patient. Make your hearts firm, because the coming of the Lord is at hand.
—JAMES 5:7–8

I can pull the weeds and till the soil and pray for rain, but I cannot force an apple to grow any faster than it will. Many precious gifts of life require steady patience and spiritual calm. In the meantime, pull the weeds, till the soil, say your prayers.

Isaiah 35:1–6a, 10
Psalm 146
James 5:7–10
Matthew 11:2–11

DECEMBER 16

*A star shall advance from Jacob,
and a staff shall rise from Israel.*
—NUMBERS 24:17

A star and a staff: these guard us and show us the way. They announce authority and light and the plan of heaven. They rest perfectly in the person of Jesus.

Numbers 24:2–7, 15–17a
Psalm 25
Matthew 21:23–27

DECEMBER 17

Justice shall flower in his days,
and profound peace, till the moon be no more.
PSALM 72:7

The psalmist speaks, not merely of regular peace but of
profound peace "till the moon be no more." This is eternal
and abiding peace. It is peace that sleeps deep and lastingly
in your bones.

Genesis 49:2, 8–10
Psalm 72
Matthew 1:1–17

⇒ 381 ⇐

DECEMBER 18

She was found with child through the Holy Spirit.
—MATTHEW 1:18

God brings life where, by human accounts, there should be none. God brings joy where, by human accounts, there should be only misery. God brings perfect healing where we expect unending woundedness, freedom where there should be only bondage, and hope where we would perceive only despair.

Jeremiah 23:5–8
Psalm 72
Matthew 1:18–25

DECEMBER 19

But the angel said to him, "Do not be afraid, Zechariah, because your
prayer has been heard."

LUKE 1:13

Poor, questioning Zechariah, made mute for his unbelief.
How often have I shrugged off the good gifts of God
because they seemed too good to be true?

God, make mute in me any voice that doubts your
generosity and your delightfully precise, personal answers
to my feeble prayers.

Judges 13:2–7, 24–25a
Psalm 71
Luke 1:5–25

The virgin shall conceive and bear a son, and shall name him Emmanuel.
—ISAIAH 7:14

By what name do you know him? "God with us," "Prince of Peace," "Wonderful Counselor"? Teacher, Father, Friend? Beloved, Lord, Messiah, Jesus? He knows you by name. By what name do you know him? By what name do you wish to know him more?

Isaiah 7:10–14
Psalm 24
Luke 1:26–38

When Elizabeth heard Mary's greeting, the infant leaped in her womb, and Elizabeth, filled with the Holy Spirit, cried out in a loud voice and said, "Most blessed are you among women, and blessed is the fruit of your womb."
—LUKE 1:41–42

How is it that an unborn child might know something we can't intuit? Maybe babies pray in ways we cannot possibly understand or remember.

This Advent, find an expectant mother who needs your extra attention and care—whether financial, emotional, or spiritual. Commit yourself to her and her child in some concrete way.

Song of Songs 2:8–14 or Zephaniah 3:14–18a
Psalm 33
Luke 1:39–45

DECEMBER 22

"Do not be afraid to take Mary . . . into your home."
—MATTHEW 1:20

These are the words of an angel, spoken in a dream. Why should anyone fear taking Mary into his or her home? What possible scandal would it be for me to make the Blessed Mother better known?

Isaiah 7:10–14
Psalm 24
Romans 1:1–7
Matthew 1:18–24

[Zechariah] asked for a tablet and wrote, "John is his name," and all were amazed. Immediately his mouth was opened, his tongue freed and he spoke blessing God.
—LUKE 1:63–64

Freedom comes in naming a thing well, naming it accurately and wholly. We are unleashed into a life of blessing when we can name and accept with our whole hearts the good gifts of God.

Malachi 3:1–4, 23–24
Psalm 25
Luke 1:57–66

DECEMBER 24

You will go before the Lord to prepare his way,
to give his people knowledge of salvation
by the forgiveness of their sins.
—LUKE 1:76–77

We grow in knowledge of God's mercy when we grow in
knowledge of our need for salvation, when we grow in
self-knowledge of our sinfulness. How we need the Lord! It
is important that we understand our own participation in
the rejection of salvation when we do not own our sins.
The more we know of this, the more of Jesus we will be
able to receive.

2 Samuel 7:1–5, 8b–12, 14a, 16
Psalm 89
Luke 1:67–79

Wednesday

DECEMBER 25

The people who walked in darkness / have seen a great light; / upon those who dwelt in the land of gloom / a light has shone.
—ISAIAH 9:2

Is it dark where you are? There's light for you, a light like no other. Though it can be shut out, it can never be extinguished. Throw open the door to all you might believe. I promise, there is Light for you.

Vigil:	Dawn:
Isaiah 62:1–5	Isaiah 62:11–12
Psalm 89	Psalm 97
Acts 13:16–17, 22–25	Titus 3:4–7
Matthew 1:1–25	Luke 2:15–20
Midnight:	**Day:**
Isaiah 9:1–6	Isaiah 52:7–10
Psalm 96	Psalm 98
Titus 2:11–14	Hebrews 1:1–6
Luke 2:1–14	John 1:1–18 or 1:1–5, 9–14

DECEMBER 26

• ST. STEPHEN, THE FIRST MARTYR •

"You will be hated by all because of my name, but whoever endures to the end will be saved."
—MATTHEW 10:22

What can we learn from this first martyrdom—that God's word is true, that Jesus wasn't lying, that the Christian life is painful and costly? We might think of it this way: when we are under attack, whatever form that might take, it may be evidence of holiness winning out. No lukewarm Christian would offer his life for something he believed in only half-heartedly. When persecution comes, turn your eyes heavenward and claim the last words of St. Stephen: "Lord Jesus, receive me."

Acts 6:8–10; 7:54–59
Psalm 31
Matthew 10:17–22

Beloved: What was from the beginning, / what we have heard, / what we have seen with our eyes, / what we looked upon / and touched with our hands / concerns the Word of life— / for life was made visible.
—1 JOHN 1:1

Jesus intends for me to have a "sense-able" experience of him: sight, sound, touch, even taste. He is made visible, accessible, available to every part of me.

Jesus, where do I find you embodied today? May I recognize you according to your will in my senses.

1 John 1:1–4
Psalm 97
John 20:1a, 2–8

DECEMBER 28

• THE HOLY INNOCENTS, MARTYRS •

God is light, and in him there is no darkness at all.
—1 JOHN 1:5

In God there is no darkness at all. None. Innocence, too, is an absence of darkness. How might I take more steps to protect the innocence around me and to build up a life of light?

1 John 1:5—2:2
Psalm 124
Matthew 2:13–18

DECEMBER 29

• THE HOLY FAMILY OF JESUS, MARY, AND JOSEPH •

Put on, as God's chosen ones, holy and beloved, heartfelt compassion,
kindness, humility, gentleness, and patience, bearing with one another
and forgiving one another.
—COLOSSIANS 3:12–13

You may have much to forgive and much to bear, but you
never have to do it alone. We bear with one another; we do
not bear anything alone. Compassion, kindness, humility,
gentleness, patience—these things do not grow in isolation,
only in community. Forgiveness can grow in community,
too. We can ask others to help us bear up under whatever
we have been given to carry.

Sirach 3:2–6, 12–14
Psalm 128
Colossians 3:12–21 or 3:12–17
Matthew 2:13–15, 19–23

DECEMBER 30

Bring gifts, and enter his courts.
—PSALM 96:8

It is not what I get at Mass, it is what I give. Do I make a gift of myself at Mass?

1 John 2:12–17
Psalm 96
Luke 2:36–40

DECEMBER 31

• ST. SYLVESTER I, POPE •

*I write to you not because you do not know the truth but because you
do, and because every lie is alien to the truth.*
—1 JOHN 2:21

You do know the truth. We would not have spent this year
together unless we both knew the truth in our own
imperfect way. Make a promise to yourself and your
Church (I will, too) to reject outright any lie about the love
of Christ that finds your listening ear: "It isn't worth it,"
"isn't real," "is only in your wounded head," "isn't available
to you," "will cost too much," "will be too painful," "will not
satisfy." You know the truth. You do.

1 John 2:18–21
Psalm 96
John 1:1–18

Also by Elizabeth M. Briel

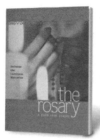

The Rosary
A Path into Prayer
$11.95 • Pb • 2024-1
Also available as an eBook

The Rosary, full of the history and practice of this great devotion, includes surprising and moving personal testimonies from the author, other devotees, and saints and holy figures, showing how rosary devotion is a practical and gratifying means of meditation that every person can use.

May Crowning, Mass, and Merton
50 Reasons I Love Being Catholic
$13.95 • Pb • 2025-8
Also available as an eBook

Briel lists 50 reasons to embrace the Catholic faith, such as daily Mass, kneelers in church, and the crucifix. With wit and great affection, covering everything from Michelangelo's creation frescoes to Pope John Paul II, this lay Catholic reminds us all why the Catholic faith is so special.

Continue the Conversation

If you enjoyed this book, then connect with Loyola Press to continue the conversation, engage with other readers, and find out about new and upcoming books from your favorite spiritual writers.

Visit us at **www.LoyolaPress.com** to create an account and register for our newsletters.

Or you can just click on the code to the right with your smartphone to sign up.

Connect with us on the following:

Facebook
facebook.com/loyolapress

Twitter
twitter.com/loyolapress

You Tube
youtube.com/loyolapress

3 Minute-Retreat

3 minutes a day can give you 24 hours of peace.

The *3 Minute Retreat* invites you to take a short prayer break at your computer. Spend some quiet time reflecting on a Scripture passage and prepare your heart and mind for the day ahead. Sign up to receive an e-mail delivered free to your inbox every morning.

Join the conversation at
facebook.com/3MinuteRetreat